Hummingbird
GARDENS

Hummingbird GARDENS

Attracting Nature's Jewels
to Your Backyard

Nancy L. Newfield and Barbara Nielsen

CHAPTERS PUBLISHING LTD., SHELBURNE, VERMONT 05482

To Skip, who always believed in me,

and to Charlotte and Aimée

N. L. N.

To the two Patricks, whose love and

encouragement helped me with this book

B. N.

Published by
Chapters Publishing Ltd., 2031 Shelburne Road, Shelburne, VT 05482

Library of Congress Cataloging-in-Publication Data
Newfield, Nancy L.
    Hummingbird gardens: attracting nature's jewels to your backyard /
Nancy L. Newfield and Barbara Nielsen.
        p.   cm.
    Includes bibliographical references and index.
    ISBN 1-881527-88-3 (hardcover)
    ISBN 1-881527-87-5 (softcover)
    1. Gardening to attract birds—North America. 2. Bird attracting—North
America. 3. Hummingbirds—North America. I. Nielsen, Barbara. II. Title.
QL676.57.N7N48 1996
598.8'99—dc20   95-51860

Printed and bound in Canada by
Metropole Litho, Inc., St. Bruno de Montarville, Quebec

Designed by Eugenie Seidenberg Delaney

Front cover photograph: Broad-tailed Hummingbird by Bob and Clara Calhoun/Bruce Coleman, Inc.
Back cover photographs: Female Broad-tailed Hummingbird by Wendy Shattil and Bob Rozinski;
Male Ruby-throated Hummingbird by Maslowski Wildlife Productions; Foxglove by Derek Fell.
Back cover illustration by Stephen A. Shurtz

Contents

Acknowledgments

A NUMBER OF PEOPLE generously contributed information, insights and ideas while we were writing this book. You will meet many of them in the following chapters. We wholeheartedly thank each for sharing with us. In addition to offering expert gardening advice, Doris Hope and Charlene Butler read chapters and reviewed plant lists. Arnette Heidcamp, Lisa Hutchins, Mary Irish and Tracy Omar examined the plant lists and made thoughtful suggestions. Tina Jones reviewed the Western Mountains chapter and sent helpful comments. Carroll Henderson, Herb Kale and Jerry Pratt contributed local plant information and other published sources that form a basis for the plant lists for each region. Staff members at botanical gardens, arboretums and other public places also helped with plant information as well. To all, we express our heartfelt appreciation.

We are also grateful to Roger Tory Peterson, who wrote the foreword to this book; to landscape architect Stephen Shurtz, who drew the garden design plans; to agent Christina Ward, for her enthusiasm for this project; and to editor Cristen Brooks, for her helpful suggestions and careful reading of the manuscript.

Nancy Newfield thanks William Baltosser, Peter Scott and Gerry Green for sharing unpublished data about the hummingbirds with which they have lived and worked. She also thanks Ron Stein and Miriam Davey for serving as important sounding boards about birds and their flowers. Their friendship and encouragement have gone far in supporting her work with hummingbirds over the years. She is also grateful to Jack and Carol Murray and Paul and Eleanor Neff for their warm hospitality during field work in Arizona.

Barbara Nielsen thanks the many gardeners and hummingbird enthusiasts who graciously granted interviews and sent follow-up information. In addition to those people featured in this book, the following led her to sources or offered other invaluable help: Michael Arnum, Anne McKee Austin, David Austin, Allen Baker, Betty Baker, Dick Beal, Janice Bradshaw, Annette Bristol, Diane Bryant, Milan Buching, Kathy Butler, Lucille Clark, Floyd Connor, Jeanette Davis, George Ellison, Elsie Eltzroth, Mitch Ericson, Herb Fibel, Steve Frye, Larry Gates, Gabriel Gauthier, Keith Geller, Laurie Goodrich, Linda Gross, Dan Guravich, Brother Hackett, Eric Hammel, Sally Harris, Wayne Hefner, Pete and Peggy Holt, Mary Hubble, Andrew Hurley, Robert W. Irion, Richard Klauke, Robert Kreba, Ruth Laney, Tony Lang, George Leslie, Russell Link, Robie Liscomb, Ellen Lyons, Carol Maurer, Mike McIvor, Brenda McKelvin, Bruce W. Miller, Jean Olah, Julie O'Malley, Patricia Mandell, Vicky Pittman, Diane Probst, Rose Pruyne, Keith Reid-Green, Mary Bridget Reilly, Chris Rimmer, Owen Roberts, Judy Rondeau, Marcus Schneck, Tom Schneider, Rob Scott, Caryn Shoffner, Norma Siebenheller, Tom Smith, Susan Stacey, Jim Thorpe, Brian Townes, Mike Turner, Rebecca Tydings, Robin Warshaw, Alan Watson, Karen Williams and Sue Wolfe.

Foreword

BY ROGER TORY PETERSON

WHILE IN MY CONNECTICUT STUDIO, I take short breaks to check on what is happening outside. I enjoy the sight of a pair of ruby-throated hummingbirds, the only pair that seems to live in our neighborhood.

I find it immensely satisfying to watch these tiny birds as they visit the trumpet vines that climb over the cedars. They may also sip from the feeder I have maintained, but they more often seek nectar from the tubular red flowers of the trumpet vine. Equally thrilling is the sight of a hummer catching insects on the wing, zooming through the air in an effortless zigzag pattern. I envy those people who have more than a single pair of hummers. Some of my friends boast of dozens, and in Arizona, even hundreds. Although we normally have only the ruby-throat in the East, western hummers are turning up as casual strays, almost always at feeders.

This book on hummingbird gardening by Nancy L. Newfield and Barbara Nielsen will show you how to attract these engaging birds to your own yard. The authors offer helpful advice to growers in every region of North America and include detailed information on the native and exotic plants that the birds prefer. They also introduce you to gardeners and hummingbird enthusiasts from Ontario, Canada to the Texas Rio Grande, as well as to the birds themselves, dazzling mites that Audubon called "glittering fragments of the rainbow."

Turk's Cap

Introduction

O NE MAY AFTERNOON more than 20 years ago, Robert Raether
planted sultan's turban, turk's cap and flowering maple in my south
Louisiana garden, showing me the basics of using natural nectar
sources to attract hummingbirds. In Louisiana's rich soil and subtropical climate, the plants flourished.

As if by magic, a hummingbird arrived almost as soon as the first bud unfurled,
although I had tried unsuccessfully to attract the birds with a feeder for more
than a year. To my delight, that first hummer, a female ruby-throat, was followed by a succession of others that darted from blossom to blossom, twittering
from dawn to dusk.

When the ruby-throats migrated south in September, I expected the show to
end. Instead, a rufous and several black-chins, then considered local rarities, arrived to brighten my winter. This unexpected bonus convinced me that nectar-
producing flowers could work far better than feeders in drawing hummingbirds,
and so I set a goal of having something in bloom for the birds throughout the year.

Very little was then known about "hummingbird gardening," as it is now
called. I began by studying the birds and the flowers that they visited throughout

North America and on their wintering grounds in Mexico and Central America. I collected much information, but many questions remained.

Which cultivated plants provided nectar? Which ones would adapt to the humid Gulf Coast climate? Which plants might be useful in my small suburban garden? Was there a difference in flower preference from one hummingbird species to another? Was there any one flower that attracted the birds better than the rest?

As I grappled with these questions, my garden became a test site. Nursery catalogs filled the mailbox. I begged cuttings from gardeners who mentioned that they had seen hummers around their yards. I collected seeds from wildflowers found on mountain hikes.

I tried almost every plant that anyone said would attract hummingbirds, though not all succeeded in my garden. Countless fuchsias, vivid in other climates, withered in our sultry southern summers. Bee balms flourished but refused to bloom. Columbines prospered for a while, before eventually drowning in one very wet year. But many tropical and subtropical vines, shrubs and perennials thrived and proved highly productive in attracting the birds.

My obsession with hummingbirds and their flowers has rewarded me with a growing network of friends who share the passion. Sometime in 1983, writer Barbara Nielsen and I met in Steve and Kathy Hope's garden in Baton Rouge, Louisiana, where I was banding ruby-throats. She had come out of curiosity with our mutual friend, the late David Hunter, and left with an armful of plants—a new recruit in the army of hummingbird gardeners. The plantings quickly took hold in her Baton Rouge garden and the

hummers followed. More than 10 years later, her unflagging interest in the birds and flowers led her to suggest that we write this book.

In researching *Hummingbird Gardens*, Barbara and I talked extensively with hummer enthusiasts across the United States and Canada. Gardeners from

Female Rufous Hummingbird at Cape Honeysuckle, Tecomaria capensis

coast to coast shared tips, observations and plant recommendations (some even sent seeds), while botanists, horticulturists, garden curators and ornithologists generously answered our questions and provided invaluable information and insights. To all of them, we are indebted.

Barbara and I hope that this book will inspire more people to discover the pleasures of hummingbird gardening. We've found that our own gardens give as much joy as the birds. Together, they bring complete contentment.

Nancy L. Newfield
Metairie, Louisiana
August 1995

9

PART I

CHAPTER ONE

Female Broad-tailed Hummingbird at Scarlet Gilia

The Hummingbird Family

*For colour shee is glorious as the Rainebowe, as shee
flies shee makes a little humming noise like a humble
bee; wherefore shee is called Humbird.*

William Wood, New England's Prospects *(London, 1634)*

HUMMINGBIRDS are one of the wonders of the New World. Early American colonists were amazed to see these small, glittering birds darting in and out of banks of wildflowers. The little fliers were so unlike the birds they knew from home, they seemed enchanted. Yet the creatures were quite real—and surprisingly tame. Settlers soon discovered that the "Humbirds," as some colonists called them, would readily visit village gardens, where they drank nectar from cultivated flowers.

In 1670, Governor John Winthrop of Connecticut described the marvel in a letter to London naturalist Francis Willughby. "I send you withal a little Box," he wrote, "with a Curiosity in it. . . . It is the curiously contrived Nest of a Humming Bird, so called for the humming noise it maketh whilst it flies."

Winthrop went on to describe the bird as ". . . exceeding little . . . and only seen

Hummingbirds like this male Anna's act as pollinators for several flowers.

in Summer, and mostly in Gardens, flying from flower to flower, sucking Honey out of the flowers as a Bee doth."

Reports circulated in Europe of an avian wonder with a weight no more than a six-pence coin and a body smaller than any known bird. Then, too, there were the hummingbird's amazing powers of flight and radiant colors. As early as 1534, the Spanish naturalist Gonzalo Fernández de Oviedo y Valdés wrote of hummers seen on Caribbean islands:

[They are] no bigger than the end of a man's thumb . . . and of such swiftness of flight that you cannot see the movement of their wings . . . The colors shine like those of the little birds artists paint to illuminate the margins of holy books.

Oviedo called the bird *pájaro mosca* (bird fly), or sometimes *pájaro mosquito* (little bird fly), a name

Female Costa's Hummingbird at Monkey Flower, Mimulus *sp.*

which led some to believe that the iridescent creatures were half-bird, half-insect.

No less fantastic were the Native American legends about hummingbirds. The Aztecs believed they were resurrected warriors, returned to the Earth to fight battles in the sky. The Maya thought that the Great God made them from scraps left over from other birds and that the sun granted them the gift of brilliant colors. The Pima tribe of the American Southwest held that the birds possessed magical powers and were able to bring both wind and rain. Other southwestern tribes, including the Hopi and the Zuni, also linked hummers with rain. They honored the rain-bearers by featuring hummingbird costumes in their ceremonial dances.

Three centuries after Oviedo first told of the curious "little bird fly," the artist and naturalist John James Audubon painted a ruby-throated hummingbird for his landmark book *The Birds of America.* In the artist's *Bird Biographies,* edited by Alice Ford,

Audubon commented on the hummer's unusual boldness—a trait that fascinates us to this day.

"The Hummingbird does not shun mankind so much as other birds generally do," the naturalist wrote. "Frequently, it approaches flowers in windows, or even flies inside rooms when the windows are kept open during the extreme heat of the day. It returns, if not interrupted, as long as the flowers remain fresh and unfaded."

The hummingbird family (Trochilidae) has more than 340 members, making it second only to the tyrant flycatcher (Tyrannidae) in the number of species with a range limited to the New World. Hummingbirds are distinguished from all other birds by their diminutive size, iridescent feathers and hovering flight, as well as by their long bills and even longer, extensible tongues. They are uniquely adapted for drinking nectar from flowers.

No fossil records remain of the hummingbird's fragile form because the fine bones of the skeleton disintegrate quickly in moist tropical climates. There is little doubt, however, that the bird first evolved in South America. Hummingbirds range from Chile's Tierra del Fuego all the way up to southern Alaska, but the number of species decreases the farther north or south of the equator you go. By far, the greatest concentration lies along the equatorial belt of South America. One hundred and fifty species are found in Ecuador alone.

Scientists believe that the hummingbird's ancestor was a small, insect-eating bird that learned to supplement its diet with nectar. It took advantage of the Tropics' bountiful supply of flowers and adapted its form to better reach the sweet liquid each blossom contained. It developed a long, slender bill and extensible tongue for probing flowers, a small body suited for maneuverable flight and powerful wings that would allow the bird to hover as it fed.

It is believed that hummingbird flowers co-evolved with the birds because hummers proved to be more reliable pollinators than insects. The tiny, long-billed birds, with their tremendous energy requirements, will busily work a bank of blossoms no matter what the weather, while insect pollinators are inactive on cold or rainy days. During the course of a single day, a hummingbird may visit 1,500 flowers!

In their bid to attract hummingbirds, the flowers on these plants developed long, tubular shapes to fit the hummingbird's bill instead of the smaller mouthparts of bees. They also shifted the color of their blooms into the red spectrum, a color easily seen by hummers but invisible to most insects, which see in the ultraviolet range. (Butterflies are an exception and are able to see red.) In addition, the flowers eliminated their fragrance, as hummingbirds have little or no sense of smell, while insects do. And, finally, the flowers withdrew the "landing platforms" commonly used by butterflies and bees, as these were unnecessary for a creature able to hover easily.

The hummingbird's reward for probing a blossom is a sweet, high-energy drink of dilute nectar (usually 15 percent to 30 percent sucrose). As the hovering bird feeds, its crown, bill, throat or chest touches the bloom's pollen-bearing anthers. Pollen collects on the bird and brushes onto the stigma of the next flower it visits, completing the pollination cycle.

Hummingbirds equipped with very long bills drink freely from a great variety of flowers. Those with shorter bills, however, must restrict themselves to plants with smaller blooms. A few are highly specialized. Their strongly curved bills enable them to reach nectar in deeply curved blossoms, which are inaccessible to other hummingbirds.

Though South America is home to the greatest number of hummingbird species, they are widely distributed throughout the Americas. They range in size from the giant hummingbird of the Andes, which measures eight inches long, to the two-and-a-quarter-inch bee hummingbird of Cuba.

So successful is the hummingbird family that the birds have laid claim to almost every New World habitat where flowers bloom. Some have adapted to harsh desert conditions, while others brighten mountain meadows or rainforests. They seek nectar at sea level and on alpine slopes as high as 15,000 feet; some even fly through occasional snows.

In North America, hummingbirds are found from coast to coast. Every region, except the Arctic and the subarctic, hosts at least one breeding species. Not surprisingly, the Southwest, which lies adjacent to tropical Mexico, is home to the greatest number of species. The variety gradually diminishes as the birds spread out from there. On the East Coast, the only nesting hummingbird is the ruby-throat; this hardy bird overwinters in Mexico and Central America, but raises its young as far north as southern Ontario. On the West Coast, the breeding range of the rufous extends into southern Alaska and the Yukon Territory.

Twenty-six species of hummingbirds have been reported in the United States and Canada, although some occur only infrequently. These include fourteen that regularly nest here; two that occasionally nest here; and ten that have been sighted throughout North America on an irregular basis.

Members of the hummingbird family are well known for their radiant colors, which are brighter than those of any other bird. Their jewellike shades run the gamut from ruby to emerald, sapphire to turquoise, topaz to amethyst. In many species, male hummingbirds are far more colorful than their mates. Scientists believe that the female's subdued plumage helps camouflage her on the nest. In the Tropics, some hummingbirds are embellished with long, showy tails, head crests and ear and neck fans, though not all sport brilliant colors. Forest-dwelling tropical hummers, called hermits, blend into the background with somber feathers of gray or brown.

Interestingly, the hummingbird's brilliant feathers contain no bright pigments. Rather, the bird's colors come from refracted light. When light strikes the flat, microscopic air bubbles within a hummingbird's feathers, it is diffracted into colors and reflects back in a flash of iridescence. This explains why the birds ap-

pear drab in the shade, yet explode into fireworks when the sun shines directly on their feathers. Their colors are determined by the thickness of the air bubbles in their plumage. Different species reflect different ranges of hues.

Like other birds, hummingbirds keep their feathers in good condition through bathing and preening. Due to their small size, they prefer shallow water, no more than a quarter-inch deep, in which they can partially submerge themselves and splash. They are also drawn to the spray of waterfalls or sprinklers and will sometimes shoot through the stream of a hand-held hose. Alexander F. Skutch in his engaging book, *The Life of the Hummingbird,* tells of a particularly winsome bather on the West Coast:

While Emerson Stoner watered his garden in California, a female Anna's hummingbird often came to

Male Broad-billed Hummingbird Leaf Bathing

flit through the spray from his hose. One day she discovered that she could ride the stream, a solid jet of water about three-quarters of an inch thick. Flying up at right angles, she alighted on the jet, as though it were a branch, and permitted it to carry her forward. Over and over she did this, apparently enjoying the stunt. She seemed to be playing rather than bathing.

In a charming ritual called leaf bathing, hummingbirds wash themselves on a leaf that is wet with dew or rainwater. Time and again, the little bird slides down the leaf, moistening its breast and shaking its feathers while still in flight. Afterward, the bather finds a spot to perch and spends a few minutes preening and rearranging its feathers.

In addition to their iridescent colors, hummingbirds are distinguished by their diminutive size. They are the smallest birds in the world, with an average weight of less than half an ounce. North America's ruby-throat, for example, weighs three grams, or about as much as a penny. The calliope hummingbird, North America's smallest, weighs little more than a dime.

Hummingbirds also have the most rapid metabolism of any bird and an average heart rate of 1,260 beats a minute. To meet their tremendous energy requirements, hummingbirds consume roughly half their weight in nectar and insects every day.

The hummingbird's flight capabilities are legendary. On near-invisible wings, beating 60 times a second, they move effortlessly: up, down, backward, forward and in place. To escape danger, the birds do a quick, agile flip, zip off upside down for a short distance, and then shoot away on a rapid retreat, a skill that sets hummingbirds apart from all other feathered creatures. Their average flight speed is 25 to 30 miles per hour, though their tiny size makes it seem much more swift. During aerial courtship displays, some males climb to a height of 75 or 100 feet and then

zoom down—using powered flight and gravity—at a speed that can reach 60 miles an hour.

Because hummingbirds appear to be constantly in motion, folk wisdom once held that they never perch. Indeed, the tiny birds are lumped with swifts in the order Apodiformes, which means "without feet." It is true that most hummingbirds do not walk or hop much, but they do perch, and sometimes sidle along a twig. At a feeder that has perches, a hummer commonly drinks heartily for 30 to 60 seconds and then shoots off for a 15- to 20-minute rest before returning to drink again. When foraging from flowers, the birds glean only a sip of nectar from each bloom. They often must visit many blossoms for each meal before flying away to rest.

Just before nightfall, hummingbirds fill up on nectar and insects, then retreat to a secluded perch. They sleep with feathers fluffed and bill pointed to the sky. On cool nights, they conserve energy by entering a state called torpor, in which the heartbeat slows, the body temperature drops and metabolism falls to a fraction of the daytime rate.

When Spaniards in the New World first observed this phenomenon, they concluded that the jewellike birds died and then miraculously came back to life. Most of these reports exaggerated the mystery of the "resurrection birds," as in this account by historian Antonio Herrera, published in 1601:

There are some birds in this country of the size of butterflies, with long beaks and brilliant plumage. . . . Like the bees, they live on flowers and the dew which settles on them. And when the rainy season is over and the dry weather sets in, they fasten themselves to a tree by their beaks and soon die. But in the following season when the rains return, they come to life again.

During a hard freeze one winter in south Louisiana, Baton Rouge hummingbird enthusiast

Female Buff-bellied Hummingbird Feeding Nestlings

O.J. Williams was able to save two rufous hummingbirds by taking advantage of their torpor. "I left the screen door open on my back porch," he recalls, "and they flew in. They perched on the screen and almost immediately went into torpor. Once they were out, I was able to pick them up and carry them over to a small storage shed, where I kept them alive with a portable heater and a couple of feeders."

The hummingbird's voice is an unusual assortment of chips, chatters and squeals. Not all have songs in their repertoire, but of the 24 species of hummingbirds that live in or visit North America, the Anna's is the most prodigious singer. Its thin, scratchy notes serve the same territory-claiming function as the throaty warbles of an American robin. Males of some other North American species also sing, but their voices have not yet been as fully studied.

When a hummingbird finds a good nectar source, it aggressively defends it from all other hummingbirds by chittering angrily and flying toward the intruder at top speed. So fierce is the competition that a male

bird may even chase off a female. The display of bravado usually intimidates an interloper, though contact is not unknown.

Unlike many other birds, most hummingbirds pair only briefly, with nesting duties left to the female. She alone will build a tiny, cuplike nest, lay and incubate the eggs and care for the young. The male's only role in the whole affair is to court the female and fertilize the eggs.

But what a courtship! As for most bird species, most male hummingbirds have far more splendid plumage than their female counterparts. Displaying males orient themselves to take advantage of the brilliant effect created when the sunlight strikes their glittering throat feathers, called gorgets.

Many males attempt to convince a potential mate of their vigor by staging elaborate courtship flights at the center of their flower-based territories. The females find their mates while foraging within the males' defended areas. The aerial patterns vary for each species. In many, the male climbs high into the air and then plummets down at a speed approaching a mile per minute. At the low point of the dive, some produce a whizzing or whining sound with specially modified wing feathers. Then they rocket back toward the sky to repeat the sequence a number of times. Some males stage these displays while facing the sun, the better to impress the female with their feathered finery.

Despite such elaborate rituals, copulation is brief. After mating, the female returns to her nearly completed nest while the male remains on his territory. He will continue to display for any approaching females throughout the nesting season.

A hummingbird's cuplike nest is a wonder to human eyes. No bigger than a walnut shell, it is woven from spider webs and plant down, then camouflaged with lichens. The female lays two eggs, each the size of a navy bean, in this cushioned nursery. Though the eggs are extremely small when compared with those of other birds, they are large in proportion to the female's body. Perhaps because of this, the mother hummingbird usually lays one egg and then skips a day before laying the other.

Incubation usually takes 12 to 14 days. When the young hatch, they are blind, naked and helpless. Their featherless bodies are about the size of honeybees and their bills are short and stubby. Bob and Martha Sargent, the only hummingbird banders who band nestlings, comment that the work is extremely difficult, as the babies' legs are so tiny and the hatchlings "wiggle so much."

The female nourishes her young with nectar, small insects and spiders. Watching the mother hummingbird feed her brood can be startling; she plunges her long, swordlike bill straight down their throats to pump in a meal. Bob and Martha Sargent report that the hatchlings respond to the humming sound of their mother's wings. "If you hum near the nest," says Bob, "up pop their heads and their mouths fly open."

Hummingbird hatchlings grow so quickly that they are ready to leave the nest, which stretches as they grow, in about three weeks. By that time, they

are fully feathered and have longer bills. They measure nearly the size of their mother, which they resemble in coloration.

For a couple of days before their first flight attempt, the nestlings prepare themselves by perching on the rim of the nest and beating their wings vigorously. Once they finally launch themselves, they soon become accomplished fliers.

Writing in 1933 in *Bird Lore*, Mary Beal tells of observing a nest of black-chinned hummingbirds:

On the nineteenth day, the babies perched on the edge of the nest and tried their wings with a quick humming motion just like Mother's, but they made no attempt to lift themselves into the air. They were still fed just as regularly as clockwork, every half hour.

The day they were three weeks old, they left the nest, flying about with a smart little air of importance, giving thin squeaks of excitement.

The mother hummingbird feeds her young for about three weeks after they have become airborne. During this transition period, the immature birds must learn how to feed themselves. They may briefly follow their mother, but also explore quite a bit on their own. Hummingbirds seen checking out peculiar "food sources"—such as a red stop sign—are often young and inexperienced. According to well-known hummingbird authority Alexander F. Skutch, such curiosity is an evolutionary advantage and frequently leads the birds to new nutritional discoveries.

The female hummingbird has little time to fret over "empty nest syndrome." After raising one brood, the mother frequently mates again and begins a second nest—and sometimes a third—before she faces the rigors of migration.

Most North American hummingbirds migrate to tropical Mexico and Central America in order to en-

Male Magnificent Hummingbird at Thistle, Cirsium *sp.*

sure a continuous nectar supply throughout the winter months. Those that live in tropical regions with year-round flowers seldom migrate, though they may wander widely as they follow peak blooms. In North America, however, the majority of hummingbirds follow a north-south pattern, with the exception of the Costa's, whose migratory movements are altitudinal, and the Anna's, which doesn't migrate in the usual sense. These birds may wander extensively in search of favored flowers. A small population of Allen's hummingbirds remains year-round on California's Channel Islands and Palos Verdes Peninsula.

The longest migration of any hummingbird is that of the rufous. This fiery-tempered, rust-colored mite nests on the West Coast from northern California on up to southern Alaska and overwinters in central Mexico's Guerrero state. From its shortest point, the journey measures 2,000 miles. The rufous is also an incurable wanderer, regularly straying during fall and winter into the southeastern United States,

and sometimes veering away to locales as distant as Maine and Russia!

Even more amazing is the migratory journey of the ruby-throated hummingbird. This emerald-backed bird spends the summer months as far north as southern Canada, yet overwinters in the tropical warmth of Mexico and Central America. While some migrating ruby-throats follow the curve of the Gulf Coast all the way down to their winter feeding grounds, the majority apparently cut the length of their trip by braving a nonstop, 500-mile flight over the Gulf of Mexico. Since hummingbirds migrate at a speed of about 25 miles per hour, the ruby-throats must beat their tiny wings for 18 to 21 hours before they reach the shore.

Countless observers have noted that migrating hummingbirds feed more frenetically than resident birds. During lean years, hungry migrants will fight over blossoms that offer little sustenance, desperate to drink what nectar they can. Particularly good plants—

such as tree tobacco in southern California or jewel-weed in the East—sometimes draw them in great mobs, where they stoke up on the sweet, satisfying fluid before continuing on their way.

In nearly all species of hummingbirds, adult males are the first to begin migration, starting with a trickle of travelers and gradually building up to a steady stream, though hummingbirds always migrate singly, not in flocks. Females follow when they've finished their nesting chores. Immatures require additional time to put on weight and perfect their flying skills. The hummer's staggered migration prevents a single disaster, such as a hurricane, from decimating an entire population.

The average life-span of a wild hummingbird is two to five years, though some have lived as long as twelve. While the hummingbird's quick, agile flight makes it difficult to catch, it has many predators. Hawks sometimes catch the birds, as do domestic cats. In Portal, Arizona, ornithologist Sally Spofford reported seeing a roadrunner prey on hummingbirds. Large insects such as dragonflies and praying mantises have been known to catch them. On more than one occasion, witnesses have seen a frog jump up and snatch a hummer in its mouth, and in California, a bass leapt out of a pond and gulped down a hummingbird that was hovering above the water. Nestlings also fall victim to everything from squirrels to opossums to fire ants.

Humans sometimes aid hummers that become entrapped in spider webs or encounter other hazards. In Arthur Cleveland Bent's classic book on hummingbirds, *Life Histories of North American Cuckoos, Goatsuckers, Hummingbirds and Their Allies*, the author records a number of such rescue attempts, including the following account by Joseph Janiec, who came to the aid of a ruby-throat ensnared in a thistle:

While I was wandering through a large hollow one June afternoon, my attention was attracted to the unusual waving of a pasture thistle. No air was stirring, and my curiosity prompted me to ascertain the cause of the movements. As I approached the thistle I noticed what I at first supposed to be a large dragonfly impaled on the prickly purple flower; closer examination, however, revealed a male Ruby-throated Hummingbird stuck to the flower, his wings not being involved in the contact but his stomach feathers adhering to the prickly, pointed stamens. Cutting off the flower, I carried it and the bird home and carefully removed the bird. Although it lost a few feathers in the operation, the little bird flew away unharmed.

Unseasonable freezes, especially during the critical northbound migration, can also take a heavy toll on those hummers whose energy reserves are already depleted. Pesticides may have an adverse effect as well, and they certainly eliminate the tiny flying insects that form a vital part of the hummingbird's diet. But the most serious threat to the birds is the destruction of their breeding habitats. Hummers most commonly nest in swamps and woodlands. Every time a forest is cleared or a swamp is drained, a breeding ground is lost to future generations. Because of this, the birds can no longer raise their young in many of the places where they were once abundant.

No North American hummingbird is endangered, though declines have been suspected in such heavily populated regions as the Northeast. This is especially true in communities that offer mostly sterile landscaping—lawns, nonflowering trees and shrubs—or acres of concrete. Gardeners throughout North America can help return hummingbirds to their yards by planting an abundance of nectar-producing flowers as well as trees and shrubs that the birds can use as shelter. Through backyard habitat enhancement, we can help ensure that these dazzlers will brighten the landscape for generations to come.

CHAPTER TWO

Red Daylily, Hemerocallis *sp.*

Plant a Hummingbird Garden

If I were to have a garden all my own, I know just
what I would plant. I would have lots of early larkspurs
and columbines and morning glories and nasturtiums.
I would plant rows and rows of caragana, pelargonium,
and tritoma; I would have no end of tiger lilies, painted
cups, bee-balms, scarlet salvias, azaleas and gladiolus;
I would train scarlet runners and trumpet vines all
over my fences; and all my shade trees would be horse-
chestnuts and buckeyes."

Arthur A. Allen, *"Rubythroat,"* American Bird Biographies

I N THE 1930S, the flower-filled garden of Mrs. Laurence J. Webster of
Holderness, New Hampshire, was a popular gathering spot on Sunday af-
ternoons. Once a week, after church, Mrs. Webster generously opened her
yard to curious visitors, who congregated to enjoy the sight of ruby-throated
hummingbirds twittering about her feeders and flowers. Naturalist Winsor Marrett Tyler, writing in Arthur Cleveland Bent's *Life Histories of North American
Cuckoos, Goatsuckers, Hummingbirds and Their Allies,* describes one such visit:

Male Broad-tailed
Hummingbird at Scarlet
Gilia, Ipomopsis aggregata

[Mrs. Webster] provided them with such a bountiful supply of food that, apparently, all the hummingbirds in the vicinity resorted to her garden throughout the summer. . . . Her garden on August 5, 1937, when Mr. Bent and I visited her, was whirring with hummingbirds—at least 40, we thought.

How did so many ruby-throats discover the banquet in this New Hampshire yard? Tyler failed to note specific plantings, although we do know that Mrs. Webster's feeders were trimmed with red. She probably also used the color in her flower beds.

Successful hummingbird gardeners from Victoria, Canada, to the Mississippi Coast have discovered that bright, bold displays of red are the surest way to attract hummingbirds to their yards. When the birds fly overhead—either on migration or in search of a meal—they spy this color from more than a half-mile away and zoom down as if drawn to a blinking "Welcome!" sign. Once in the garden, the tiny birds investigate the nectar supply and check to see if there are bushes and trees to provide them with shelter and an advantageous perch.

The hummingbird's almost magnetic attraction to red has been well-documented. Countless observers have noted that *anything* red may draw a hummer's attention, from a gardener's red cap to the stripes on an American flag. The birds inspect such items hoping to find the red, nectar-rich flowers that provide them with food in nature. In a 1909 account of an Alaskan expedition, biologist Joseph Grinnell had this to say about a rufous hummingbird's dogged search for a meal on Admiralty Island:

> " . . . [a male rufous] buzzed about some bright red tomato cans that had been thrown out. Stephens records that at the same place, May 2, a male came around camp investigating everything that was red, such as a red-bordered towel, the red places on the end of a fruit box, an empty salmon can, and particularly a red bandana handkerchief hanging on a bush; this the bird went to three times."

Some hummingbird enthusiasts, knowing of the birds' fondness for red, rely on scarlet-trimmed feeders to attract hummers to their yards. But the best way to draw a greater number of birds—and to encourage some to stay—is to include a combination of feeders and nectar-producing plants in your landscape design. Otherwise, a hummer may buzz through your garden on a brief visit, but fly off in search of a more ample nectar supply. This is particularly true of those hummingbirds (a small percentage) that never learn to use feeders; to such individuals, your oddly shaped red gizmos may be just as disappointing as empty tomato cans.

But even the most dazzling displays of color won't draw hummingbirds if your flowers bloom at the wrong time of year. Your first step, then, in designing a successful hummingbird garden is to familiarize yourself with your region's hummingbirds. Ask such questions as: Which species are commonly found in my area? When do they migrate? When and where do they nest? Can I expect winter strays or a year-round population? (We'll help you answer these questions in later chapters.) Then choose your plants so that some catch the eye of passing migrants early in the season, while others unfurl their blossoms later. The idea is to provide a succession of flowering plants throughout the time that you can expect the birds. Your feeders should be filled and waiting, too, so when a hummer zips down to check out the bright colors it has spotted from up high, it will find plenty of food.

Some gardeners enjoy almost instant success in attracting hummingbirds. This is particularly true for those who live along major flyways or near nesting areas. Pam Perry, a biologist in Brainerd, Minnesota, experienced this in her own yard. "I put a feeder out in the spring of '83, and hummingbirds were there within 10 minutes," she says. The birds have returned every spring since and remain on her property throughout the summer.

Others patiently tend both plants and feeders for weeks—or even months—before spotting an iridescent flash of green. If this happens to you, be persistent. Once the birds discover a well-planned garden, they will return year after year. In fact, if you are late hanging out feeders, you may see a tiny creature hovering in place where a feeder *used to be!*

Be prepared, too, for periods when the birds mysteriously vanish, only to return a few weeks later. This sometimes happens because they are feasting on an abundant natural food source. In the eastern United States, for instance, ruby-throats frequently disappear from backyard gardens when Japanese honeysuckle blooms. This nectar-rich vine grows rampantly in woodlands and fields and is one of the ruby-throat's favorite foods. When the bounty declines a month or so later, the diminutive birds return.

Similarly, many females desert feeders and gardens during the nesting season. The mothers need to feed their young a high-protein diet, so they search out a plentiful supply of insects. Gardeners who live in a city with an aggressive mosquito-control program rarely enjoy nesting hummers in their yards, while those with such insect-producing features as a swamp or a pond often host more than one hummingbird family.

The availability of large trees and shrubs nearby also plays a role in the number of hummingbirds you attract. Newly created subdivisions that lack mature trees do not draw as many birds as more woodsy settings. Trees and shrubs provide the birds with shelter and good perching spots and are the foundation of any garden. If your property lacks such plantings, choose a variety of species—a few that will be in bloom when the first hummingbirds arrive and others that will flower later in the season. Shade trees such as oak, cypress and sycamore are also useful in a hummingbird garden. Although the trees may take years to reach full size, keep in mind that you are planning for the future—yours and the hummers'.

Hummingbird gardening is part of an overall trend to restore contact with nature in our daily lives. By planting to attract hummers, we can soften the stressful effects of contemporary urban society—and help the birds at the same time.

Begin your hummingbird garden by thinking carefully about your yard's framework (that is, the large, permanent plantings such as trees and shrubs). You may find it helpful to make a sketch of your existing garden and work out plans from there. Add trees as needed, then generously fill in empty spaces with masses of flowering shrubs, vines, annuals and perennials. Even if your garden is already well established, you can easily add hummingbird flowers to existing beds. In general, place tall flowering plants in the back of a bed and shorter ones to the front so that the birds can more easily maneuver to reach the blooms. To ac-commodate the maximum number of hummers, use vine-covered lattices and large, dense shrubs to create visual barriers in your yard. This will allow more than one bird to set up a feeding territory within a small space.

When selecting plants, choose flowers that will catch a hummingbird's eye with that irresistible color red and its close relatives, pink and orange. Brighten garden beds and borders with bold splashes of these colors and add more sources of nectar with potted plants, window boxes or hanging baskets. Use vines to decorate fences, trellises or nonflowering trees. Naturalized wildlings such as salmonberry or sultan's turban will bring a taste of the forest to your more civilized setting. Numerous nurseries now specialize in native plants, or the plants can be obtained through a local native plant society. The statement your garden should make is, "Food! Lots of food! Stop off here!"

Staggered blooming times will help you keep your yard alive with the birds. A gardener in Portland, Oregon, for instance, may welcome migrating rufous hummingbirds by planting red-flowering currant, an early-spring bloomer that is highly attractive to the birds. Later in the season, that same gardener could plant such summer-bloomers as bee balm, red-hot-poker, fuchsia, foxglove and coral bells. In late summer and fall, cardinal flowers, scarlet sage and phlox could round out the floral display while supplying fall migrants with an ample food supply. And finally, viburnum, Oregon grape and winter-blooming camellias could provide nectar for any year-round Anna's hummingbirds.

While vivid floral displays will draw hummers in the first place, the birds won't stay unless they are rewarded with food. Keep in mind that while most classic hummingbird flowers are red, pink or orange, the blossoms usually have a tubular shape and are unscented as well. Biologists believe that fire pink, trumpet creeper and other hummingbird flowers with these characteristics probably co-evolved with the nectar-drinking birds. Choose red flowers first, followed by pink, orange, purple, blue and yellow. If

Male Anna's Hummingbird at Cape Honeysuckle, Tecomaria capensis

given a choice of shades, choose the brightest. White should be your last choice, with the exception of Japanese honeysuckle and a few other nonconformists.

Japanese honeysuckle is an excellent hummingbird plant; ruby-throats prefer its sweet nectar to feeders. Yet this variety of honeysuckle has fragrant, creamy white and yellow blooms. What's more, it is an introduced plant, brought to North America from Japan during the 19th century. But none of that matters to the birds. They have discovered that the vine's hundreds of tubular flowers drip with nectar; when it blooms, hummingbirds whirl around it like a cloud of high-strung bees.

In the West, another nonnative plant, tree tobacco, has a similar draw. When this lanky shrub blooms with hundreds of pale yellow flowers, Anna's and rufous hummingbirds abandon backyard feeders. Wise

gardeners will find a way to include at least one of these favorites in their yards.

Other plants may *seem* perfect for hummingbirds. Flowers such as roses, geraniums and sweet William have conspicuous red blooms but produce little nectar. Hummingbirds will inspect the plants but won't return if the yield is disappointing. This is also true of many cultivated hybrids. Although the wild versions of these flowers produce ample nectar, their showier cultivars, which were developed for color or form, may offer little food because nectar production is not a characteristic for which most plants are bred.

For maximum effectiveness, consider the number of blossoms on the plant and the length of the blooming season. A bush or vine that produces hundreds of small, nectar-filled flowers over a long period of time is a far better choice than a plant with only a few large blooms. Although both morning glories and four-o'-

clocks draw hummingbirds and can be highly effective in a hummingbird garden, they unfurl their petals for relatively brief time periods. Blossoms that remain open throughout the day are more useful.

Each region of North America has hummingbird plants that work especially well in that area, and those that do not. In later chapters, we will help you discover those that are best suited to your location. We will also give you tips on the flowers that the birds in your area prefer. Spotted jewelweed, that ruby-throat favorite, is an excellent choice for eastern gardeners, but its love of damp, shady places rules it out for drier parts of the West. Similarly, that desert beauty, ocotillo, would not thrive in a humid Gulf Coast yard.

Most hummingbird plants require little fuss or maintenance, which is good for the gardener and the hummingbirds. It is vitally important to avoid using insecticides and fungicides, particularly systemic ones, in your hummingbird garden because the poisons may be carried into the nectar. Use fertilizers sparingly, if at all. Many gardeners have found that a well-balanced garden—home to birds, toads and other wildlife—is relatively pest-free. If insects do get out of hand, control the problem with insecticidal soap.

As interest in hummingbird gardening grows, an increasing number of nurseries have started to stock suitable plants. If you have difficulty finding the plants you want, check the mail-order sources in the back of this book. You may also wish to contact a native plant society (most states and provinces have these) or a nearby botanical garden. Finally, your local chapter of the National Audubon Society may be able to put you in touch with other hummer enthusiasts, who are often willing to share seeds, cuttings and their backyard hummingbird show. Indeed, sharing with like-minded individuals is one of the prime pleasures of a hummingbird garden.

To some hummingbird gardeners, flower beds artfully planted with a hummingbird's natural food source are the most satisfying way to attract the birds. Flowers are much easier to care for than feeders: you don't have to wash, scrub or sterilize them, and you never have to worry about changing the solution. Plants also harbor small insects, an essential part of the hummingbird's diet. But beyond these practical concerns, it is thrilling to watch the birds forage for food as they would in nature. As a hummingbird works a garden bed, you are better able to appreciate its amazing powers of flight. It darts in to drink deeply from a blossom, hovering on a blur of wings. Then it backs up and shoots to the side before zipping in to feed on the next blossom. After sipping from a dozen or more flowers, the hummer streaks off as quickly as it came.

As thrilling as it is to watch the birds in your garden beds, you'll probably find that a combination of feeders and flowers will bring you the most success. The use of feeders will allow you to support a greater number of hummingbirds, especially during migration, when dozens of them may whiz about a single garden. Those hummingbirds that have learned to use feeders know that they offer a quick, reliable meal.

Bob and Martha Sargent, who garden for the birds in Trussville, Alabama, say that migrating ruby-throats usually disregard their flowers in favor of feeders. "You're limited only by the number of feeders you have," says Bob Sargent, "especially during migration."

Part of the reason that Mrs. Laurence Webster's 1930s garden attracted so many hummingbirds is that she was one of the first to use feeders. She was inspired to do so after reading in *National Geographic* of Margaret Bodine's successful experiments with feeders on the porch of her Maine home in the 1920s. Mrs. Webster started out with pill bottles filled with a sugar-water solution, but found them hard to maintain as her hungry contingent of hummingbirds quickly drained the vials. She eventually commissioned a local glass-blower to create larger, inverted bottles especially for her garden.

In describing his visit to Mrs. Webster's yard, Winsor Marrett Tyler noted that many of the ruby-throats that flashed about her garden seemed quite tame.

"[Mrs. Webster] accustomed the birds to associate the sound of her voice with the presence of food and often called them to a vial she held in her hand by whistling the 'phoebe' note of the chickadee . . . [During my visit with Mr. Bent] she covered the scattered feeding tubes and, seated at an open window beside Mr. Bent, who held a filled tube in his hand, gave the chickadee call. A bird came up out of the garden, poised a moment, then alighted on Mr. Bent's finger."

Mrs. Webster and others who made their own sugar-water vials would no doubt be astounded by the number and variety of hummingbird feeders now on the market. Even in the 1970s, such feeders were a rare item, sold mostly through specialty catalogs. Today, however, they are widely available and come in a bewildering assortment of styles.

In choosing hummingbird feeders for your garden, look for those that are durable, easy to clean and attractive. Select glass or clear plastic, so you can easily see when the solution is low or looks cloudy, and make sure each feeder is trimmed with enough red to catch a hummingbird's eye. If you draw a number of hummingbirds to your garden, choose large feeders over small ones. At times when the activity drops, you can "downsize" by filling them only partway.

Despite their diminutive size, hummingbirds are fiercely territorial. They refuse to share a food source with another bird unless there are so many hummers vying for a meal that it becomes impossible to drive them all away. Extraordinary numbers like this most frequently occur after the young have fledged or during migration. To prevent a single hummingbird from dominating your garden, you might hang two or three feeders in your yard, a minimum of six feet apart and ideally out of sight of each other. (As mentioned earlier, lattices and large shrubs can help separate your garden into feeding territories.) Another equally effective strategy is to cluster your feeders together so that one bird cannot guard them all.

Hang at least some of your feeders in spots where you can see them from a porch or through a window. Although hummingbirds usually zoom off to a favorite perch after they sip nectar, they do not seem afraid of drinking from feeders in the open, where you can more easily view them. Unlike shier birds, they readily visit window-side feeders and pay scant attention to people on the other side of the glass. They also dart up to feeders on porches, decks and patios. If you select feeders with perches, the birds will frequently sit as they drink and give you an even better look.

When people first began feeding hummingbirds, many prepared a honey-water solution, reasoning that honey is a "natural" food. While it may be natural for bees, it is not appropriate for hummingbirds—and may even harm them.

The sugar in honey is chemically different from that in nectar. Honey is a simple dextrose sugar while nectar is a sucrose-fructose compound. What's more, honey spoils quickly when dissolved in water, and the bacteria and molds that grow in the spoiled syrup can make hummingbirds ill.

You can easily make a solution nearly equivalent to natural nectar by dissolving one part cane sugar in four parts boiling water. (Boil the water first, measure it and *then* add the sugar, so you don't lose water through evaporation and end up with a concentrated mix.) After the syrup has cooled, fill your feeders. You can store any leftover solution in the refrigerator for about a week.

Knowing of the hummingbird's fondness for red, many people add red food coloring to their solution, but the color is not necessary, as the red parts on feeders effectively attract the birds. Equally unnecessary are the artificial nectar solutions now on the market. Not only are they much more expensive than homemade sugar-water, but their promises of "needed protein and minerals" are misleading. Wild hummingbirds get all the nutrients they need through nectar (both natural and otherwise) and insects.

Foxglove, Digitalis *sp., attracts* hummingbirds *in several regions.*

In order to keep the hummingbirds coming, the feeders should be well maintained. Hummingbirds will shun a bitter or sour solution, so you should change the mix in your feeders at least once a week. In very hot areas, you may need to do so daily. You will know the solution has spoiled when it begins to look cloudy or moldy. One sip and the hummingbirds will know it, too. How disappointing to spy a hovering bird in your garden, only to watch it streak away after a single drink from a neglected feeder.

To clean your feeders, take them apart and rinse in warm water. If you see any mold, use a small, flexible brush to scrub it off. Stubborn mold can be killed by soaking the feeders in one part bleach to ten parts water. Scrub as needed. Afterward, rinse all parts thoroughly and allow them to air-dry. Most hummingbird enthusiasts find it convenient to have two sets of feeders. While one batch is soaking or drying, the other can be filled and hung in the yard.

Feisty hummingbirds sometimes scold gardeners as they take down feeders. This is particularly true of the rufous hummingbird, which is notorious for its aggressive personality. To avoid a confrontation with a particularly territorial hummingbird, some people wait until dark to swap feeders.

Others have reported that their backyard hummers seem to recognize them, and that individual birds will zoom up in anticipation when they step outside with a filled feeder. Jo Houghton of central New York says that ruby-throats regularly drink from a tray of feeders in her hands when she walks outside to hang them.

Perhaps even more surprising are the hummingbirds that boldly seek nectar from hand-held bouquets. Mildred Broadbent of Park Rapids, Minnesota, experienced this when she picked some gladiolus in her garden. "Suddenly, I heard the whir-r-r of a hummingbird," she recalls. "As I stood and watched, he went over every flower in my arms. I was thrilled to be that close to him."

Joyce Mohr of Tisdale, Saskatchewan, had a similar encounter while holding some wild bluebells. "I had just picked a handful, and a ruby-throat came and drank from them, right before my eyes!" she says. "Needless to say, I haven't picked any since. Now I leave them for the hummingbirds."

Many gardeners have discovered that a dripping or misting water source will attract hummingbirds. Although the birds obtain all the drinking water they need from nectar, they do need water in order to bathe. In nature, they often clean their feathers by streaking in and out of the fine spray of a waterfall; or they dip and splash in a shallow stream. Chester C. Lamb, writing in 1925, describes bathing by a number of Xantus' hummingbirds in Mexico's Baja California:

> At one place the hummingbirds' bath was discovered, where a trickle of water flowed over a flat rock a short distance and then dropped in a tiny waterfall. At one time I counted nine birds at once taking a bath. They would sit in the water and give themselves a thorough shower with their wings; then, to finish off, they would fly against the falls, breast first, and then they would back up to the falling water. Besides the birds busily bathing, there were as many more sitting around on the bushes, drying themselves.

You can provide bathing facilities for your hummers by keeping a very shallow pan filled with water. The pan should have a narrow rim so that the birds can perch before entering the water, which should be no more than one-quarter inch deep. A sprinkler or mister also encourages bathing, especially on a hot, dry day. If placed so that the water splashes on nearby foliage, you may be treated to the sight of a hum-

mingbird leaf bathing. Avian Aquatics Inc. of Lewes, Delaware, specializes in water sources for backyard birds. The company makes a "Leaf-Mister" especially designed for birds that prefer to bathe on wet leaves. Co-owner Sally Fintel notes that in her own garden, the ruby-throated hummingbirds are particularly fond of bathing on the leaves of autumn olive (*Elaeagnus umbellata*) and silky dogwood (*Cornus amomum*) although they will use the leaves of other plants as well.

Hummingbirds also find birdbath dripper attachments highly attractive. Both drippers and misters can be equipped with timers set to go off in the morning or late afternoon, thus reducing the amount of water used. A mister turned on high squirts out only about three gallons of water per hour, while a dripper can be set to use only a pint per hour.

To the surprise of many gardeners, other birds such as orioles, house finches and woodpeckers sometimes visit hummingbird feeders. Ants, wasps and bees are also attracted to the sweet solution, as are other rarer visitors, including anole lizards, squirrels, opossums, bats and raccoons. Those who live in more wooded areas have even observed nectar-guzzling bears. In 1992, a couple participating in the Cornell Laboratory of Ornithology's Project FeederWatch reported that a black bear ambled up to their backyard deck in rural Ohio and proceeded to chug-a-lug the sweet syrup from a feeder! As amusing as some of these invaders may be, they rob hummingbirds of their intended food and may chase them off as well.

You can solve many of these problems by fitting bee guards over your feeder's ports. Bees and other birds are unable to drink through the guards. Another way to stop bees, at least temporarily, is to move the feeder a few feet away. This will confuse them into thinking the food source is gone, though sometimes it is necessary to remove the feeder entirely for a while. If you enjoy orioles in your yard, hang out "oriole feeders" in a separate area because these larger birds, which also drink nectar, often discover that hummingbird feeders provide an easy meal and can drive hummers away with their aggressive behavior.

Though relatively new on the market, these feeders are sold in specialty shops and through mail-order catalogs. A separate hummingbird feeder, set on a stump to prevent it from swinging wildly when the orioles leave, works just as well.

To control wasps, hornets and yellow-jackets, hummingbird banders Bob and Martha Sargent make

Clustering feeders can prevent any one hummingbird from dominating the food supply.

homemade traps. They begin by removing the wrappings from an empty, two-liter soft drink bottle. Next, they cut four nickel-sized holes in each side, about halfway up. Then they pour about four inches of spoiled feeder solution into the bottle and add a chunk of raw meat (such as roast) and a piece of fruit. Finally, they add a few drops of liquid detergent to the mix and hang the bottle in the garden. The scent attracts the unwanted insects, which fly in but then can't fly out because the detergent coats their wings. The Sargents recommend changing the mix once a week, and using the traps only as needed.

Squirrels not only drink sugar-water, but gnaw on feeders. You can generally outwit these clever rodents by hanging the feeders with monofilament fishing line or relying on the same sort of baffles that

are sold for use with other bird feeders.

To halt the steady march of an ant column, smear cooking oil, petroleum jelly or mineral oil on your feeder's hanging wire. Larger ants can be stopped by fitting an ant moat—a cup filled with water—over the wire. Several innovative companies now offer feeders with a moat built into the center of a saucer-shaped disk. They are designed so that rainfall will overflow and drain from the cup, rather than spilling into the feeder solution.

If night-raiding opossums, bats or raccoons become a problem, take your feeders down at nightfall and hang them out again in the morning until the mammals have given up on that food source. Bears can be thwarted by hanging the feeders out of reach with a cord and pulley system.

One final comment needs to be made about feeders, and that concerns the persistent myth that keeping your feeders up in the fall will prevent hummingbirds from migrating. This is simply not true. In those hummingbird species that migrate (and not all do), the birds' departure time is based on the length of the day, *not* the abundance of food. Indeed, when the time to migrate comes, the urge to leave is so powerful that no amount of food could persuade them to stay. The confusion about this probably arises from the fact that some other types of birds may tarry at an easy food source.

We recommend that you leave your feeders up at least one week beyond the date when you last saw a hummingbird. That way, any stragglers will be able to refuel. Indeed, biologists note that those hummingbirds that lag behind in migration are invariably weak and undernourished. By leaving your feeders out, you may give such a bird the boost it desperately needs—and you may even save its life.

CHAPTER ONE

Hedgehog Cactus, Echinocereus engelmannii

California

When winter approaches, the other California hummingbirds withdraw into Mexico, . . . but [the] Anna's [hummingbird], relieved of competition, darts about the California gardens all winter long, visiting even the smallest garden in the heart of town.

Roger Tory Peterson, 1948, Favorite Audubon Birds of America

MORE THAN 35 YEARS AGO, Louise Blakey of Los Altos, California, began experimenting with plants to attract hummingbirds to her yard. At the time, such a practice was virtually unknown, so Blakey patiently relied on trial and error. Today, her yard is a hummingbird paradise—almost completely filled with flowers except for walking trails—and gardeners from coast to coast seek her advice.

Blakey is a small, enthusiastic woman who generously shares both seeds and cuttings from her garden. She credits much of what she knows about hummingbird flowers to Whiz, an injured Anna's hummingbird that was entrusted to her care. Whiz was unable to fly and became so tame that he would perch on Blakey's finger and allow her to carry him to blossoms in her garden. This gave Blakey a

Immature male Anna's Hummingbird

unique opportunity to study his reaction to the plants that she was testing in her yard.

"If Whiz didn't like a particular plant, he wouldn't feed from it again," says Blakey. "He taught me a lot about which plants hummingbirds like. I took him to other gardens too, and I took detailed notes about the flowers that he preferred.

"Some friends had a garden with flowering tobacco [*Nicotiana alata*] for example, which many peo-ple believe is a good hummingbird plant. Whiz wouldn't have anything to do with it. He also helped me discover that some fuchsias are better than oth-ers. Many of the hybrids, for instance, are not good nectar providers."

With the help of Whiz—and the hundreds of other hummingbirds that have worked her bountiful flower beds over the years—Blakey has compiled a list of "25 Outstanding Hummingbird Plants." Though

31

the choices reflect the observations of a gardener in the San Francisco Bay area, Blakey notes that many of these plants work extremely well in other West Coast locations. Some can even survive temperatures of 15 degrees F or below.

Of all the plants in her garden, Blakey finds that her hummingbirds are especially fond of *Fuchsia lycioides,* which produces tens of thousands of small red and purple blooms throughout the year. *Fuchsia magellanica* is also popular. Salvias (*Salvia* spp.) are favorites, especially pineapple sage, Mexican bush sage and anise sage. The Anna's hummingbirds feed so constantly on the fall- and winter-flowering pineapple sage that Blakey features several large stands of this in scattered locations throughout her yard.

Among native plants, Blakey's top choices include woolly blue-curls (*Trichostema lanatum*), red-flowering currant, honeysuckle penstemon (*Penstemon cordifolius*), California fuchsia and tree mallow (*Lavatera assurgentiflora*), which produces a plentiful crop of rose-colored flowers all year.

She also highly recommends red-hot-poker (*Kniphofia uvaria*), bee balm *(Monarda* spp.), Mexican cigar or shrimp plant (*Justicia brandegeana*), impatiens, cardinal climber (*Ipomoea multifida*), the South African heaths (*Erica* spp.) and the Australian grevilleas (*Grevillea* spp.) especially the 'Robyn Gordon'.

Rounding out the list are a number of other "very choice" plants, including such hummingbird staples as bottlebrush, tree tobacco (*Nicotiana glauca*), flowering maple and eucalyptus.

Given that hummingbirds originated in South America and have gradually spread northward, it is not surprising that California has the greatest number of species on the West Coast (seven, counting the broad-tailed, which is usually only sighted in the state's eastern mountains). Throughout this region, almost anyone who gardens for hummingbirds is sure to be rewarded with the sight of one or more of these iridescent creatures hovering in the yard.

Many California residents have turned to drought-tolerant plants for their hummingbird gardens because of water-conservation regulations. One such enthusiast is Charlene Butler, who lives in a dry, brushy area, known as chaparral, just north of San Diego. At any one time, at least a dozen Anna's swoop through her flower-filled yard, which is set on a hill overlooking the San Pasqual Valley. From spring through fall, she also spots Allen's hummingbirds, which probably nest in the nearby scrubland. Costa's and rufous hummingbirds are rarer visitors, although both turn up occasionally.

Butler credits hummingbirds with inspiring her to garden in the first place, more than 20 years ago. "I was living in San Jose at the time and there was a large fuchsia just outside my kitchen window," she recalls. "Every morning a beautiful Anna's would come and feed on it when my daughters and I were having breakfast."

Butler was so intrigued with the emerald visitor that she read everything she could about hummers. Soon afterward, a friend introduced her to Louise Blakey, who led her on a guided tour of her own hummingbird garden. Butler says that the visit "opened whole new vistas" for her. It showed her what a hummingbird garden *was* and what to plant in one. She left filled with inspiration—and with cuttings to add to her own yard.

Today this avid gardener is a trustee of the Quail Botanical Gardens, a hummingbird haven in nearby Encinitas. She also gives slide shows on landscaping for the birds, with an emphasis on plants able to withstand extended dry spells. "My goal is to get at least one hummingbird plant in every yard," she says.

In her own garden, Butler's favorites include the grevilleas, a family of shrubs native to Australia. "They can take high heat and require a minimum amount of water," she says. "Some of them bloom year-round. I have a 'Robyn Gordon' that has been in bloom solidly for two and a half years. It has attractive, large blossoms that are a pinkish rose and the hummingbirds are always on it."

She also recommends bottlebrush (*Callistemon* spp.), another Australian native. Butler has several va-

*Male Allen's Hummingbird
at Twinberry Honeysuckle,*
Lonicera involucrata

rieties in her yard in white, pink and red. "They have flushes of bloom, and when they're in bloom the hummingbirds go nuts."

Butler says the hummingbirds also feed on her Cape honeysuckle (*Tecomaria capensis*), which she has allowed to grow rampant along a cyclone fence. "They also like my natives and my perennials; and my buddleia, my tree tobacco and the correas [a type of Australian shrub]. I also have a large salvia collection, which they regularly visit."

In addition to drinking nectar, the hummingbirds feast on the gnats attracted to Butler's fruit trees (which she doesn't spray), and when she has a sprinkler going, the birds fly through the spray to clean their feathers.

As in Butler's yard, the hummingbirds that seek nectar in the nearby Quail Botanical Gardens are drawn to a number of dry-climate, imported plants, including the grevilleas, kangaroo paw (*Anigozanthos* sp.) and eucalyptus, all from Australia, and several

kinds of South African protea (another flowering shrub). In addition, the birds are extremely fond of the fuzzy pink flowers of the Australian bottle tree (*Brachychiton bidwillii*). "When they're in bloom, this is one of the best places in the garden to see hummingbirds," says Butler. "The hummers fight like crazy over them."

In spring, aloe plants (*Aloe* spp.) in the garden's Old World Desert section provide a feast for the hummingbirds. The plants require very little water yet supply a copious amount of nectar. Blooms range from pale cream to salmon, orange, tricolored and even green. Other good viewing spots at Quail include the fuchsia garden and the annual and perennial beds.

Many California gardeners have discovered that a trickling water source proves irresistible to hummingbirds, particularly during a prolonged dry spell. Once, during an evening visit to Quail, Butler saw an Anna's hummingbird jump in and out of a water-

Male Costa's Hummingbird at Aloe flower, Aloe sp.

fall that had just been turned off. Only a trickle of water was running down, so Butler assumed the bird was catching insects; but then she noticed that it would aim its little body directly for the drips. After bathing, the hummingbird preened its feathers on a nearby branch.

Just to the south, in San Diego, the resident Anna's hummingbird is absolutely abundant throughout the year, while the Allen's and rufous migrate through. Although both of the latter visit feeders and gardens during their northward journey, biologist Philip Unitt of the San Diego Natural History Museum says he most often sees them refueling on the yellow blooms of the tree tobacco. "That's the granddaddy for them," he says. "It's native to South America and thrives in disturbed soils. It's all over the place here—even in vacant lots. I can't imagine how the rufous and Allen's managed to migrate through before it was introduced."

More wooded areas of the city, especially along creekbeds, attract black-chinned hummingbirds in small numbers in the summer months. San Diego's other regular visitor is the Costa's, which has a migratory pattern unlike that of any other hummingbird.

Unitt, who has studied the bird in that part of the state, says that it resides in the desert in late winter and early spring, where it feeds on flowering plants such as ocotillo and chuparosa. Then in April, it ascends to nearby mountain meadows, where it feeds on alpine flowers such as Cleveland sage (*Salvia clevelandii*) through early July. Then it moves again, this time heading for feeders and gardens in San Diego. It remains locally abundant through the fall, then abruptly disappears—back to the desert to repeat the cycle.

Interestingly, Unitt has found that in the mountains and foothills of San Diego County, the Costa's thrives in half-recovered burnt chaparral areas. "The four most abundant plants in those areas are *Penstemon spectabilis,* which has big purple flowers; woolly blue-curls; sticky nama (*Torricula peria*) and slope semaphore (*Mimulus brevipes*), a type of monkey flower," he says. "The first three that I named have purple flowers. We found that those four plants dominated this half-recovered area and that the Costa's hummingbird was the most abundant bird there. So it appears that chaparral fires, which are a natural occurrence, actually benefit the Costa's."

The Costa's nesting season runs from February through April and coincides with the wildflower bloom in the desert. Anza-Borrego Desert State Park, a two-hour drive northeast of San Diego, is an excellent place to see the Costa's at that time of year. Other hummingbirds commonly found in the park include the Anna's, which remain year-round, and the black-chinned and rufous, which migrate through.

Ranger Bob Theriault says that two native plants are the big hummingbird attractors in the park: chuparosa, which means "hummingbird" in Spanish, and ocotillo (*Fouquieria splendens*), which has hundreds of tubular, fire-red blooms. He reports that the birds also like manzanita (*Arctostaphylos* spp.) and, at higher elevations, penstemon. "Those are definitely their favorites," he says, "but I've seen them poke their bills into all kinds of things."

Theriault recommends the park's Tamarisk Grove Campground as an especially good viewing spot during nesting season. At least 10 or 12 Anna's nest in the tamarisk trees around the campground, and the trail to Yaqui Wells and the Cactus Loop, which both lead off from there, offer excellent sightings, too. "You'll see Costa's nesting all along the trails," he says, "usually in desert lavender [*Hyptis emoryi*]."

Two other public places in the San Diego area are worth noting. They are the hummingbird aviary in the San Diego Zoo and the hummingbird pavilion in its sister facility, the Wild Animal Park. Both showcase exotic tropical species such as the violet sabrewing, the sparkling emerald and the black-throated mango. After a full day of walking through the zoo, it's soothing to sit on a bench in the secluded aviary and watch an elegant fork-tailed woodnymph hover inches from your head to sip from feeders or flowers.

In heavily populated Los Angeles, private gardens provide needed habitat for hummingbirds. Backyards with flowering plants and feeders never fail to attract at least one Anna's hummingbird, and other species often show up as well. The area's public gardens also play a vital role, providing both food and shelter. One such refuge for hummingbirds is the Tucker Wildlife Sanctuary, set south of the city in hilly Modjeska Canyon.

The sanctuary began as the retirement home of Ben and Dorothy May Tucker, who experimented with hummingbird feeders as early as 1926. Their first efforts were with shot glasses, which they filled with sugar-water and set in a row on their porch railing. Later, they designed some feeders with large, inverted bottles similar to those on the market today. Soon hummingbirds from the nearby chaparral had discovered the Tuckers' "hummingbird bar." Dozens of them whirred up for drinks of artificial nectar within a few feet of the couple, who sat on an observation porch to enjoy the sight.

During a 1930s visit, naturalist Roger Tory Peterson marveled not only at the feeders, which were extremely rare at the time, but also at Mr. Tucker's clever use of a fluorescent spotlight, which brought out the full iridescence of the visiting birds.

After Mrs. Tucker died in 1939, the property was donated to the then California Audubon Society, which opened it to the public as a nature reserve. During World War II, when sugar was rationed, the sanctuary was granted special permission to buy the substance for their hummingbird feeders.

Today, dozens upon dozens of hummingbirds—including Anna's, black-chinned, Costa's, Allen's, rufous and an occasional calliope—may be seen in the 12-acre sanctuary, depending on the season. Manager Ray Munson says that the birds frequent the reserve's chaparral area in spring and summer, where they feed on such plants as monkey flower (*Mimulus* spp.), mountain lilac (*Ceanothus arboreus*), woolly blue-curls, manzanita, tree tobacco, penstemon, chaparral honeysuckle (*Lonicera interrupta*) and gooseberry and currant bushes (*Ribes* spp.). Then in fall and winter, they move to the reserve's oak and riparian (streamside) areas and seek nectar at the two dozen feeders. "That's the best time for viewing them on the observation porch," says Munson. "There are fewer flowers then, so the birds are driven in to the feeders."

Another excellent spot to view hummingbirds in greater Los Angeles is the Rancho Santa Ana Botanical Garden in Claremont. Henry E. Childs, Jr., author of *Where Birders Go in Southern California,* says the garden attracts a significant number of the birds because, "It's an island of vegetation in suburban Los Angeles, which is very heavily populated. It's a large green space surrounded by a sea of dwellings."

Rancho Santa Ana features a profusion of native California plants arranged by habitat—desert flowers, mountain flowers, riparian flowers and so on. Because of the variety of plants, something is always in bloom, a worthwhile goal for any California gardener.

Nan Moore, a docent at the garden, notes that the Anna's hummingbird is "all over" Rancho Santa Ana throughout the year. She estimates that at least 100 Anna's nest on the property. They treat visitors to their courtship flights as early as December and on through March; and some of the females build their nests along heavily walked trails. One year a particularly tame Anna's nested in a mahonia shrub about five feet from the ground. She didn't pay any attention when Moore stopped by with groups of curious school children. "She would stay right on the nest," says Moore, "and sometimes she would let us watch her feed her young."

The Costa's hummingbird is also fairly common at Rancho Santa Ana. Not surprisingly, this desert dweller mostly hangs out in the desert section, where it prefers to survey its territory from the top of a tall yucca (*Hesperaloe* spp.). Ray Wells, who leads Audubon Society walks through the garden, suspects that the Costa's nests at Rancho Santa Ana, as does the black-chinned, though neither raise their young in such conspicuous spots as the Anna's. During spring and fall migration, both rufous and Allen's flash about the preserve, although the rufous is far more common.

Both Wells and Moore hang feeders for hummingbirds in their own yards, as do many area residents. Anna's and black-chins are their most common visitors. Wells notes that the Anna's can become quite tame, buzzing within inches of his head when he works outdoors. Interestingly, Wells reports that both the Anna's and the black-chins desert local feeders in March and don't reappear until June. Yet they remain abundant at Rancho Santa Ana, where numerous flowers are in bloom. This is probably due to two factors: the hummers forsake the feeders in favor of the botanical garden's bountiful supply of nectar, and the nesting females are off collecting insects for their young.

Some residents manage to keep female hummers from departing by setting out banana peels or other fruit just before and during the nesting season. The scraps attract fruit flies, which provide the females with the extra protein they need to raise their young. Ray Munson, manager of the Tucker Wildlife Sanctuary, experimented with this on his own property and was rewarded with three nesting hummers—two Anna's and a black-chinned—the first year.

Yet another major oasis in greater Los Angeles is the 130-acre Huntington Botanical Gardens, which attracts the same species as Rancho Santa Ana. "You can see hummingbirds here at any time of year," says curator Clair Martin. "Where they are in the gardens depends on the blooming cycle. Of course, they're attracted to red tubular flowers, but they go to other colors, too. We have some blue-flowered agapanthus, for example, that they love. When it's in bloom from late spring through early summer, they feed constantly on that."

Martin notes that other hummingbird favorites include the gardens' many varieties of bottlebrush and flowering maple, as well as the large collection of winter-blooming African aloes. Around the time when the aloe stop flowering in February or March, the cacti unfurl petals in the desert section. The desert bloom continues throughout the summer and attracts a significant number of hummingbirds during that time. One visitor who strolled through that section on

Male Black-chinned Hummingbird at Lantana Flower, Lantana *sp.*

an August day found it "swimming with hummers."

Farther up the coast, Joan Hardie's five acres near Santa Barbara draw squadrons of hummingbirds in summer and fall. "By August there are so many hummers it's like a busy airport out here," she says. "I go through three gallons of sugar-water every day."

Hardie lives in a hot, dry chaparral area in the mountains outside of town. She has left most of her property in boulders and sagebrush, though she does grow hummingbird plants, especially drought-resistant natives, closer to the house. In spring, the hummingbirds feast on the bountiful wildflowers in the surrounding countryside. When the blooming season ends, they pour into Hardie's yard by the hundreds, mobbing the 14 feeders hung along her deck.

"They become so bold that they'll drink from the feeders as I'm carrying them out to hang," she says, "but it's nice to know that when natural nectar is available, they'll go to that."

In addition to seeking out artificial nectar, the chittering birds perch and feed on a large mimosa (*Albizia julibrissin*) tree under Hardie's deck and buzz around beds of salvia and native penstemon. They're also fond of the monkey flower that grows wild on Hardie's property, as well as woolly blue-curls. The black-chins in particular fiercely defend a nonnative *Echium* 'Pride of Madeira' shrub, which shoots out tall spikes covered with blue flowers. (Other California gardeners note, however, that bees cover the *Echium* so completely that hummers are unable to feed.)

Another highly attractive feature in Hardie's yard is a trickling, two-foot man-made brook that recycles water. On hot, dry days, hummingbirds sit on the edge of the brook's rock ledge to bathe. Bolder individuals fly up to Hardie when she waters the garden with a hose. They wash their feathers by taking a quick zip through the spray.

Hardie's yard is such a hummingbird thoroughfare that she has attracted seven species. Anna's are the most common and live on her property year-round. During the dry season, which runs from August through October, their numbers easily top 200. A smaller number of these birds raise their young on Hardie's property, sometimes nesting in unusual spots. One year, an Anna's built her minuscule nest on top of a clothespin.

Black-chinned, rufous, Allen's and Costa's are Hardie's next most common visitors, in order of abundance, and the shy calliope ventures into view about once every spring. Rarest of all was a broad-billed hummingbird, which remained on her property for three days.

In town, at a lower elevation, the Santa Barbara Botanic Garden is also a hummingbird sanctuary. Anna's are abundant in the garden throughout the year and raise their young there. Allen's and black-chins nest on the property, too, though in smaller numbers.

Chuparosa, Justicia californica

Horticultural assistant Florence Sanchez suspects that a fourth hummingbird, the Costa's, nests on the site as well. "They're usually thought of as a desert hummingbird, but we have a small coastal population," she says. "Nesting has never been confirmed, but they're here during nesting season, so it makes me wonder."

The garden's final hummingbird is the aggressive rufous, which takes up temporary residence during spring migration. "When they're here, you know it," Sanchez says. "They chase off everything in sight." The rufous does not return to the garden in the fall, as it typically follows inland mountain ranges during its journey southward.

The 65-acre garden concentrates on California natives. It features more than 1,000 plants and five miles of walking trails. Although hummingbirds may be seen throughout the property, Sanchez particularly recommends an April or May walk along the Porter Trail, which leads through a section of chaparral plants. She notes that several species of native penstemon, in pink, magenta and blue, are planted in that area. "I've seen hummingbird wars there among Costa's, black-chins and Anna's when they're in bloom," she says.

Other top hummingbird favorites along the Porter Trail include red bush or climbing penstemon (*Penstemon cordifolius*) and California fuchsia (*Zauschneria* spp.). A separate section with many different kinds of manzanita also draws the birds, which feed on the insects these plants attract as well as their nectar. In late winter and early spring, California gooseberries and currants bloom in several sections of the garden, and the hummingbirds concentrate there. Sanchez has also seen them feasting on island bush snapdragon (*Galvezia speciosa*), native columbine (*Aquilegia* spp.) and several varieties of salvia, as well as on desert flowers such as scarlet bugler (*Penstemon centranthifolius*) and chuparosa.

The botanic garden sells many of these plants in its nursery so that visitors can create similar habitat in their own yards. Sanchez notes that California natives do best when planted in the fall.

Perhaps the best place in California for viewing Allen's hummingbirds is the 150-acre Arboretum at the University of California, Santa Cruz. Set on a bluff overlooking Monterey Bay, the Arboretum has a worldwide reputation for its extensive collection of Australian and South African plants but also features a large area of California natives.

As is true in most of the state, the Anna's hummingbird is a year-round resident at the Arboretum, though its numbers drop each spring when the smaller, but much more aggressive, Allen's migrates in. The first of the Allen's arrive in mid-January, and their numbers steadily build through the end of March.

"They just seem to take over," says biologist David Suddjian, who leads birding tours through the Arboretum. "In late March and early April, you can see 75 to 100 Allen's on a walk through the Arboretum, especially males. You'll see a lot of displaying and a lot of chasing."

Most thrilling for visitors are the Allen's elaborate aerial courtship displays, which often take place right along a trail. In fact, Suddjian notes that it's common to watch multiple courtship flights in the Arboretum, as the flowers attract such a high density of birds. In addition to the Allen's, a smaller number of rufous migrate through before continuing on to nesting sites as far north as Alaska. Costa's, black-chinned and calliope hummingbirds are rarer visitors. When they do turn up, it's usually during migration.

Suddjian says that while hummingbirds are found throughout the Arboretum, perhaps the biggest concentration is in the Australian section. "They especially seem to like the Australian grevilleas, which have abundant, tubular flowers," he says, "and the correas, Australian plants that look similar to penstemon." He notes that the hummingbirds also regularly feed on other Australian imports, including the Arboretum's more than 30 varieties of bottlebrush, some of which have green or purple flowers, blue gum (*Eucalyptus globulus*) and proteas (*Protea* spp.).

It's worth emphasizing that a surprising number of Australian plants are highly attractive to hummingbirds, in addition to being drought-tolerant and pest-resistant. Indeed, many bear the characteristics of classic hummer plants, with tubular red flowers, little or no scent and lots of nectar.

In the Arboretum's native plant section, the hummingbirds feed on the many varieties of penstemon, in addition to the columbines, gilia and manzanita. Suddjian says that, historically, manzanita was the principal winter food source for the Anna's and Allen's hummingbirds, which are early nesters. "The Anna's nest as early as December and sometimes have their first brood fledged by January or February," he says. "There's a progression of different species of manzanita that bloom from late winter through the spring, and the birds have probably adapted to that progression. The Anna's is probably able to pull off that first, early brood because of the manzanita."

Suddjian notes that the many different kinds of native currant and gooseberry in the Arboretum have staggered blooms, too, and are thought to play a similar role.

Blue gum, an Australian import, also provides the Anna's with a winter food source. It is fairly numerous in the Arboretum as well as in many other parts of coastal California. This large tree, which produces thousands upon thousands of pale yellow blooms, begins to flower in December and reaches its peak in January, when the Anna's is raising its first brood. Biologists believe that the widespread introduction of this tree has probably helped increase the Anna's population.

In chaparral areas with mostly native vegetation, the Anna's still rely heavily on manzanita, which flowers even in dry years. Norma Mastin, who lives on a 1200-acre ranch in the San Joaquin Valley, says that her resident Anna's each stake out a territory around a manzanita bush when it is in bloom. The plants' staggered blooming times provide the birds with food from winter through spring. In fact, Mastin says that when she rides across the ranch and hears an Anna's singing, she's nearly always able to find the bird in a flowering manzanita.

California lilac (*Ceanothus* spp.), another native shrub, also provides food for the hummingbirds on

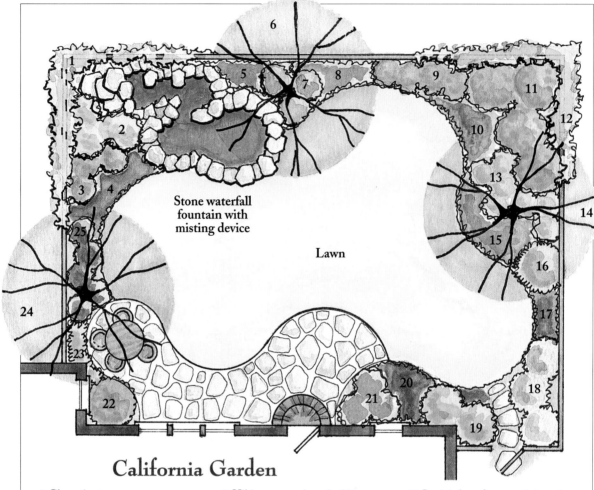

California Garden

1. Clematis *sp.*
2. Ceanothus arboreus *California lilac*
3. Chaenomeles speciosa *flowering quince*
4. Justicia brandegeana *Mexican cigar*
5. Mirabilis jalapa *four-o'clock*
6. Grevillea robusta *silk oak*
7. Salvia leucantha *Mexican bush sage*
8. Impatiens wallerana *impatiens*
9. Hibiscus rosa-sinensis *Chinese hibiscus*
10. Fouquieria splendens *ocotillo*
11. Callistemon *sp. bottlebrush*
12. Lonicera sempervirens *coral honeysuckle*
13. Anigozanthos *sp. kangaroo paw*
14. Malus baccata *flowering crab-apple*
15. Salvia guaranitica *anise sage*
16. Erythrina crista-galli *cry-baby*
17. Justicia brandegeana *shrimp plant*
18. Buddleia alternifolia *butterfly bush*
19. Abutilon pictum *flowering maple*
20. Pentas lanceolata *pentas*
21. Penstemon cordifolius *honeysuckle penstemon*
22. Hibiscus syriacus *althaea*
23. Canna *sp. canna lilies*
24. Albizia julibrissin *mimosa*
25. Justicia californica *chuparosa*

Mastin's ranch. Like the manzanita, it is drought-tolerant. Mastin says that it flowers despite lack of rainfall, although the blooms don't last as long. The variety that grows on her ranch is commonly known as buckbrush (*Ceanothus fendleri*). It can grow quite dense and thorny and features white blossoms, which appear in late spring or early summer.

Native wildflowers are yet another food source. Mastin says the hummingbirds are "all over them" when they bloom in spring and summer. The birds especially like the penstemon, but diligently check out all other flowers that might contain nectar.

In the nearby Sierra foothills, Betty Randall and her husband, Bob Potts, enjoy watching hummingbirds feed on their property, which sits at an elevation of 2,800 feet. Their 20-acre spread is set in a pine-oak woodland, which they have left natural save for a fenced-in area close to the house. Every year, both Allen's and rufous hummingbirds pass through during spring and fall migration, and Anna's hummingbirds live on their property year-round.

"Many people say that the Allen's migrate north only along the coast," says Potts, "but that's not true. We have Allen's here every spring, not tremendous numbers, but always a few. And we attract two or three or four rufous at a time. During fairly wet cycles we have black-chins, but that hasn't happened for a while."

The migrating birds drink heavily from the couple's three feeders. They also visit the several varieties of buddleia planted close to the house, as well as the Australian grevilleas. "The grevilleas are a real catnip to them," says Randall. "They don't need much water, and they bloom over a long period of time."

Randall says that neighbors all along the ridge landscape for hummingbirds and hang out feeders, thus providing the birds with a steady supply of food.

Some of the most remarkable hummingbird sightings in California take place during spring and fall migration. This is especially true when hundreds, or even thousands, of the famished birds stop off to feed in a single spot.

Ray Wells, who leads tours for the Pomona Valley Audubon Society, witnessed such a gathering in Ventura County. "I once saw swarms of hummingbirds feeding on some tree tobacco that was growing all along a ditch," he says. "I've never seen so many hummingbirds! There must have been *thousands* of them. In fact, there were so many hummingbirds at first I thought they were bees."

Henry E. Childs, Jr., who lives near Los Angeles, felt similar amazement when he visited a friend about 75 miles east of the city center, in a desert region near Big Morongo Preserve. "It was late August," he recalls, "and rufous hummingbirds were migrating through. My friend had at least 10 feeders up, and the rufous were stacked up *five deep* to one hole.

"Even though they're normally very aggressive," Childs said, "they were not chasing each other. It was early in the evening and they were obviously tanking up at the end of the day. They were just like planes lined up at the airport, waiting for their turn to take off."

While a concentration of migrating hummingbirds is an unforgettable sight, many California gardeners find the everyday pluckiness of the Anna's hummingbird just as extraordinary. These nonmigratory birds are year-round residents in many yards and thus become accustomed to the people they see on a regular basis.

Gardener Charlene Butler, for instance, says that the Anna's that live on her property fly up to "chat" at her when she works in the yard, twittering from only a foot away. "Once, one even bumped into me," she says. She also notes that when she stands outside with the hose, the fearless little birds hover in the spray.

Anna's hummingbirds have *landed* on Joan Hardie on more than one occasion. One morning, she walked onto her deck wearing a red robe and a female flew up and perched on her shoulder. "She took one look into my eyes and was gone," Hardie says. "It was as if she said, 'What am I doing here?'"

Some Anna's show such tolerance of people that they build their nests outside kitchen windows or along busy walkways. One particularly fearless mother raised her young in a small tree in an open-air mall, paying scant attention to the shoppers strolling by.

Hummingbird observer Robert S. Woods, writing in 1940 in Bent's *Life Histories*, had this to say about the Anna's charming boldness:

> **Their tameness cannot reasonably be attributed to mere stupidity, but rather to justified confidence in their own agility and swiftness, and perhaps also in human good will, since their power of discrimination is shown by their noticeable wariness toward cats. In their disposition and temperament hummingbirds are hardly comparable to any other birds but remind one most strongly of chipmunks.**

It is partly this appeal that makes the Anna's, and other hummingbirds, so welcome in our gardens.

CHAPTER TWO

Crimson-flowered Currant, Ribes sanguineum

The Pacific Northwest

The main body of the Rufous Hummingbird migration arrives just as the crimson-flowered currant (Ribes sanguineum) is bursting into bloom, and of the flowers of this shrub the hummingbirds are especially fond. At that time every bush is alive with the darting hummers, and it is one of the most brilliant bird and flower spectacles of the West.

Leslie L. Haskin, Oregon, writing c. 1940 to Arthur Cleveland Bent

IMAGINE A FIERY-THROATED BIRD, about twice the size of a bumblebee, flying all the way up from Mexico to nesting grounds as far off as the Yukon Territory and Alaska. This is the phenomenal journey that the rufous hummingbird makes every spring—a migration that may cover 3,000 miles. The flashy little rufous is a common backyard visitor in the Pacific Northwest. Every spring it returns to set up territories throughout the region, behaving more like an airborne viking than a worn-out vagabond.

Biologist Mark Hixon of Oregon State University has studied the rufous for more than a decade. He has great admiration for the bird's survival qualities, which include a keen intelligence and a blazing temper. "They're absolutely amazing

Male Rufous Hummingbird at Scarlet Gilia, Ipomopsis aggregata

animals," he says, "starting with their migration."

Hixon and his colleague, Lynn Carpenter of the University of California at Irvine, have found that the rufous sets off on migration when it weighs about five grams. It will fly nonstop as far as its fat reserves will take it, a distance of about 500 miles.

"It stops to rest and refuel when its body weight reaches a low of 3.5 grams," says Hixon. "It can be quite aggressive at that stage, especially if there are a lot of other hummingbirds to compete with."

The rufous hummingbird will remain at its stop-off point for about two weeks, resting and feeding heartily on nectar and insects. During that time, its body weight will return to a plump five grams before it takes off on the next leg of its journey.

"That's an increase of almost 50 percent in just two weeks!" says Hixon. "And then it repeats the process."

Every spring, gardeners throughout the Pacific Northwest await this long-distance traveler, whose sudden, blazing appearance brings a surge of excitement to the garden. "From early March on, people have rufous, rufous, rufous at their feeders," says Fred Bowen of coastal Oregon. "The rufous is *the* hummingbird in local yards."

Many gardeners easily attract eight or ten or even two dozen rufous at a time during migration, especially those who hang more than one feeder and plant eye-catching stands of red-flowering currant (*Ribes speciosum*) or salmonberry (*Rubus spectabilis*). Scientists believe that these shrubs co-evolved with the rufous, because their blooms are precisely timed to the bird's spring arrival. Throughout the Pacific Northwest, mobs of the migrants are rare, but they do occasionally happen. Biologist Rich Hoyer, a long-time resident of Corvallis, Oregon, recalls seeing swarms of migrating rufous along a road that cuts through some marshland in the state's Klamath County. "It was late August and *hundreds* of rufous were feeding on blooming bull thistles [*Cirsium vulgare*] along a five-mile stretch of road," he recalls. "There were so many of them, they were like insects. You could get out of your car and sit by a thistle plant and they would come and feed just inches away. It was one of the most amazing sights I've ever seen."

On other occasions, Hoyer has observed groups of 25 to 30 migrants darting around a single black locust tree (*Robinia pseudoacacia*), whose white blossoms produce prodigious amounts of nectar.

Another hummingbird enthusiast, Harry Nehls of Portland, has also witnessed such gatherings. "When the rufous arrive in Oregon, they usually stop along the southern coast, where a number of plants and shrubs are blooming," he says. "You may see *hundreds* of them gathered around one plant. They don't just feed on flowers, either. I've seen them work over the fresh growth on coniferous trees. The tips are coated with a sweet liquid. I've tasted it myself. It's a thin coating of a sweet juice, although I wouldn't call it sap."

Whirling clouds of the rufous even occur in southeastern Alaska. Steve Heinl of Ketchikan recalls watching 30 or more migrants buzzing around feeders in the coastal town of Hyder and 15 to 20 vying for nectar at some backyard feeders in Haines. He notes that the migrants are less numerous on Ketchikan, which sits on an island, but that he easily spots five or ten in a day.

While the rufous is certainly the most common hummingbird in the Pacific Northwest, it is by no means the only one. The closely related Allen's hummingbird nests along the southern Oregon coast, while the glittering, rose-helmeted Anna's has recently expanded its range northward into Oregon, Washington and British Columbia and regularly visits Alaska. (This is probably linked to the spread of suburban gardens.) East of the Cascades, the calliope returns each spring and remains through the summer. Other, less numerous species in the region include the black-chinned, as well as such occasional visitors as the broad-tailed and the Costa's.

If you live in the Pacific Northwest, you should plan your hummingbird garden so that rich sources of nectar are available when the migrants arrive in spring. While early-spring bloomers will certainly attract the birds to your yard, summer flowers will encourage some to stay for the nesting season. An abundance of such plants as hardy fuchsia (especially *Fuchsia magellanica*), Cape fuchsia (*Phygelius capensis*), California fuchsia (*Zauschneria* spp.), honeysuckle, penstemon, cardinal flower (*Lobelia cardinalis*), columbine (*Aquilegia* spp.) and red-hot-poker (*Kniphofia uvaria*) will entice the tiny birds to your garden throughout the summer. Feeders, of course, also play a role in attracting hummingbirds, as do trickling water and mature trees and shrubs in which the birds can nest or perch.

The Anna's hummingbird presents a special challenge to area gardeners. This essentially nonmigratory bird remains in parts of the Pacific Northwest throughout the winter, where it ekes out a living from feeders and the shrinking supply of nectar and insects. If you would like to attract the Anna's—and you live

Sap from sapsucker wells is another source of energy for this male rufous hummingbird.

within its range—you should maintain your feeders year-round and plant a selection of fall- and winter-blooming flowers. Depending on your location, these include such choices as witch hazel (*Hamamelis virginiana*), hardy fuchsia, bottlebrush, vestia, winter-blooming camellia (*Camellia sasanqua*), viburnum, strawberry tree (*Arbutus unedo*) and winter jasmine (*Jasminum nudiflorum*). Hanging flower baskets can be brought outside on warmer days.

Ben and Lola Gardner, who live near the Pacific Coast in Pistol River, Oregon, successfully attract both rufous and Anna's hummingbirds to their yard. Their property encompasses about 70 acres, much of it left wild with native spruce and pine trees, a few Douglas firs and "lots and lots" of nectar-producing huckleberry (*Vaccinium* spp.), salmonberry and twinberry bushes, as well as white-flowered madrone trees (*Arbutus menziesii*). Their blossoms, wrote Leslie L. Haskin in a 1940 letter to Arthur Cleveland Bent, "are perfect honey pots."

Rufous males begin to appear in the Gardners' yard in late February; the first females follow about two weeks later. By April and May, the brilliant, rust-colored birds are absolutely abundant on the Gardners' property, and some remain throughout the summer. During that time, the Gardners' Anna's hummingbirds move off. They remain scarce until August, returning only after most of the rufous have started their southward journey.

Early in the spring, the rufous feed heavily on native flowers. Later, they move closer to the Gardners' house to work the extensive plantings. These include such hummingbird staples as penstemon, honeysuckle (*Lonicera* spp.), heather (especially *Erica* spp.) and South African dierama (*Dierama* spp.), a bulb in the iris family that produces delicate tubular flowers in lavender, pink and white.

In addition, the rufous show a marked preference for the 20-odd Chilean flame trees (*Embothrium coccineum*) that flourish in the Gardners' yard. Their vibrant red blooms bring in hummers for about six weeks in June and July.

"The blossoms are a fire-engine red and they come out in clusters," says Lola Gardner. "When they're in bloom you'll see mobs of rufous, at least 20 at a time, chasing and dive-bombing each other around those trees. It's quite a sight to see their flashy colors against those bright red blooms."

Several Australian flame trees (*Telopea oreades*), which flower at the same time as the Chilean ones and flower again in fall, attract the hummers as well. But Ben and Lola note that the rufous especially mob the *Embothrium*, which is larger.

Another key hummingbird plant in the Gardners' yard is fuchsia, which flowers almost continuously in coastal Oregon's mild, foggy climate. Ben and Lola plant the hardy red and purple variety as well as the pink. They note that fuchsia will die back during a severe frost but will grow again from its roots. Some of the bushes in the Gardners' yard have become quite large, about 10 feet wide and nearly as tall. When in bloom, each bush unfurls thousands of blossoms.

"We have a big one like that by our kitchen window that the hummingbirds visit a lot," says Lola. "That's the only way I'll wash dishes—I love to watch the hummingbirds as I work."

Three or four Anna's hummingbirds spend the winter on the Gardners' property, where they regularly visit the feeder that the couple maintains. The Anna's also rely on the fuchsia bushes, as well as on a South American shrub called vestia (*Vestia lycioides*), which grows about 10 feet tall and produces yellow, tubular flowers.

"The vestia is kind of skittish in its blooming cycles, but it does bloom in winter," says Lola. "It provides food for the female Anna's when they're raising their young."

Another hummingbird gardener in coastal Oregon is Fred Bowen, who lives on 20 hilly acres in Gold Beach. Like Ben and Lola, he has planted a large flower garden on the acreage close to his house but left the rest of his property in native vegetation.

He attracts rufous, Anna's and the occasional Allen's.

"The rufous hummingbirds always arrive when the salmonberry is in bloom," says Bowen. "Salmonberry is a very common native plant that grows at the edge of forested areas, in cleared areas and along roadbeds. It produces a flower that's an inch across and a deep purple-red. When it begins to flower, I think to myself, 'The rufous will be coming soon,' and within a day or two, they do."

Bowen says the rufous is also highly attracted to red-flowering currant, which blooms at the same time, and to native gooseberry (*Ribes sanguineum*). "But they seem to prefer salmonberry and red-flowering currant," he says. "The currant attracts a lot of insects, plus it provides nectar."

Like the Gardners, Bowen has found that hummingbirds are magnetically drawn to his fuchsia bushes, which are an important winter food source for the Anna's. Bowen also recommends bottlebrush (*Callistemon* spp.). He has one with bright red flowers that blooms every couple of months throughout the year. Another of his favorites is red-hot-poker, which flowers from spring into the summer.

"The red-hot-poker has small, tubular blooms and the hummingbirds go from one little flower to the next," Bowen says. "They'll spend a fair amount of time on each stem."

Although most people find the rufous to be more aggressive than the Anna's, Bowen has observed the opposite in his yard. He says that during migration, six or eight rufous will "kind of line up" to drink from his feeder in the mornings and evenings—a tolerance he has never witnessed in the Anna's. He has noticed, however, that the Anna's disappear from his yard when the rufous arrive in spring. As at the Gardners', they don't reappear until August, after most of the rufous have set off for Mexico.

A little farther up the coast, near Oregon's Cape Arago, hummingbirds work the blooms in the botanical garden at Shore Acres State Park. The Anna's lives in the garden year-round; rufous and Allen's stop by during migration.

"You'll never see swarms of hummingbirds, but you'll see them chasing each other," says staff member George Guthrie, "and you'll easily see three or four or five on a walk through the garden."

Just as other gardeners have reported, Guthrie says that the winter staples of the Anna's are hardy fuchsia and lemon bottlebrush (*Callistemon citrinus*). Other preferred plants in the garden include such hummingbird standards as red-hot-poker and cardinal flower. "Those are their favorites, although they drink from lots of other plants," says Guthrie. "They'll even fly through the open doors of our greenhouse to feed on the flowers inside."

Red-hot-poker, Kniphofia uvaria

The Allen's hummingbird, which nests each year in the southern part of coastal Oregon, is a close relative of the rufous. Though it ranges as far north as the state's Cape Blanco, it is most reliably seen in Azalea Park in the city of Brookings. There, female Allen's hide their tiny, cup-shaped nests in thickets of azalea bushes, many of which have reached a height of 15 feet. The birds feed from a number of plants in the park and the surrounding area. These include azaleas (*Rhododendron* spp.), salmonberry, Himalaya

berry (*Rubus procerus*), red-flowering currant, wild manzanita—especially hairy manzanita (*Arctostaphylos* spp.), honeysuckle and madrone trees.

Colin Dillingham, a biologist with the United States Fish and Wildlife Service, lives just five houses down from Azalea Park. Both Allen's and rufous hummingbirds swarm to his yard during spring migration. The Allen's remain to nest and raise their young, while the rufous move on to breeding grounds at higher elevations. An additional three or four Anna's enliven his garden year-round.

Dillingham says that red-flowering currant is one of his most valuable hummingbird plants. It blooms from early March through April and is always "hit hard" by migrating Allen's and rufous, which begin to arrive at about that time. The hummingbirds also drink from the several varieties of fuchsia in his garden, as well as from honeysuckle, flowering twinberry and Himalaya berry bushes. In winter, the Anna's regularly visit his backyard feeders.

Angeline Cromack of Corvallis, Oregon, also cites red-flowering currant as a top hummingbird plant. "It's a real winner," she says. "If you plant red-flowering currant, you'll be able to attract the rufous when they're first returning and setting up their territories."

Cromack also hangs two hummingbird feeders, one in front and one in back of her house. "I hang them out of sight of each other so that one dominant male doesn't take over," she says. "However, when the rufous first arrive, I've had three perched at the feeder, drinking, and two others hovering about. When one would take its bill out, another would stick its in while still in flight!

"Later in the year, when they're setting up nesting territories, they're much more aggressive and chase each other off. I once had a calliope venture into my yard, but it was only able to take a few sips before a male rufous came roaring up and drove it off."

Cromack especially recommends red-hot-poker,

Female Allen's Hummingbird at Butterfly Bush, Buddleia *sp.*

whose blooms also attract orioles; hardy fuchsia, especially *Fuchsia magellanica*; hanging baskets of single-flowered *Fuchsia* 'Marinka'; coral bells (*Heuchera sanguinea*); columbine and viburnum, which flowers in early February and provides food for the Anna's.

Another key feature in Cromack's garden is a dripping attachment to her birdbath. "We've had our birdbath for 20 years," she says, "but the hummingbirds didn't use it until we added that.

"The water drips out of this curved copper attachment and then spills over the edge of the bird bath. I've seen female and immature rufous hummingbirds sit on the concrete edge where the water is slightly overflowing and bathe there.

"Before we had that, the hummers would sometimes bathe by sitting on an azalea leaf, directly under the spray of a stationary sprinkler. It's dry here in summer, and I've found that water can be a real attractor."

In the yard of another Corvallis resident, Mary

Fran Sewell, newly fledged youngsters appear by the end of June. They soon learn to feast on a backyard bounty that includes California fuchsia, red-hot-poker and other flowering plants.

"Last year we had a lot of youngsters," says Sewell. "You could tell they had just left the nest because they seemed so lost—they didn't know what to do. We have a security system near the door with bright red and yellow stickers, and they kept going back to that. They just *knew* there had to be something good there!"

Gardeners in nearby Salem, Oregon, also attract migrant rufous. Jerry Smith says that they appear in his garden for several weeks each spring and then move off to nest in the more rural, wooded areas outside of the city. He notes that hummingbird enthusiasts in those areas can easily attract a dozen or more at a time.

"Their visits to urban yards like ours are sporadic during nesting season," Smith says, "but then, after they've fledged their young, we'll suddenly see a number of immature rufous in the garden. They'll hang around for a few weeks and drink from the flowers we've provided—hardy fuchsia, butterfly bush (*Buddleia alternifolia*), columbine, honeysuckle, coral bells—and then they'll head off on migration."

Smith says that the young rufous are just as aggressive as their parents. Not only do they squabble with each other, but they chase off finches and other birds two and three times their size.

A little farther to the north, in Seattle, Washington, the first rufous males usually appear in mid-March; the females begin to arrive about two weeks later. An abundance of native salmonberry provides these early migrants with a bountiful supply of food, as do feeders in local yards. Nectar in the weeks to follow comes from an assortment of garden flowers, but wilder areas lure them, too. For instance, uncultivated areas in Seattle's Discovery Park offer a profusion of nectar-filled native plants such as orange honeysuckle (*Lonicera ciliosa*) and madrone trees.

The 534-acre park is Seattle's largest and provides food for hummers throughout the year. Naturalist Penny Rose says that Anna's live in the park year-round, while the rufous return in spring and remain through August.

According to Rose, spring is the best time for viewing the tiny birds, especially along the park trails. "There's lots of salmonberry there," she says. "It blooms in early March, right when the rufous are returning. If you time it right, you can see the male Anna's singing and the rufous males doing their courtship displays. It's quite a sight."

On sparsely settled Whidbey Island, northwest of Seattle, dozens of rufous return each year to Hummingbird Farm in Oak Harbor. Owner Dave Harry and his staff grow about four acres of flowers for drying. They also plant two large display gardens and four theme gardens, including one for hummingbirds. "We have lots of color here," he says, "and that attracts the rufous. In fact, we see so many we named our business the Hummingbird Farm."

Harry says that when the rufous arrive in mid-March, they mainly feed on the native currant and salmonberry in the surrounding countryside. On the flower farm, they also seek out the early bloomers. They also regularly drink from the property's three feeders, which are hung at scattered locations.

"We'll have as many as 12 rufous at a time around one feeder," says Harry. "We have one that's hung right off the front of the building, and they visit that. It's amazing how bold hummingbirds can be. They'll drink from that feeder even with people around.

"This happens in our display gardens, too, where people wander through to look at plants. The rufous will zip right around them to visit the flowers. They don't seem at all afraid."

The rufous visit many, many flowers on the Hummingbird Farm, but seem particularly fond of hardy fuchsia, French honeysuckle (*Hedysarum* spp.), Hall's honeysuckle (*Lonicera japonica*), foxglove (*Digitalis* spp.), coral bells and several sages (*Salvia* spp.).

The demonstration garden at Hummingbird Farm is not the only one in Washington State. In recent years, the Washington Department of Wildlife has sponsored six such gardens throughout the state. Among these is a combination hummingbird and butterfly garden in Spokane's Manito Park and Botanical Gardens.

Because Spokane lies east of the Cascades, its climate is drier than that to the west. Not surprisingly, the hummingbirds in eastern Washington are different, too. They include the rufous, calliope and a smaller number of black-chins. The Anna's, which are so common on the coast, visit on rare occasions.

Although the Manito Park garden was partly designed for butterflies, it features a number of plants that are attractive to hummers. These include eastern and western red columbine, tricolored bugle weed (*Lycopus americanus*), prairie fire penstemon (*Penstemon* sp.) and dwarf blazing star (*Liatris* sp.).

A second Department of Wildlife-sponsored garden lies in the western part of the state. This one is set in Bellevue, at the Lake Hills Greenbelt Ranger Station. Ranger Barbara Jordan says that everything in the garden appeals to hummingbirds. "Our red-flowering currant blooms early and offers food for the rufous when they first arrive," she says. "And we have lots of other flowers that bloom later on.

"One of their favorites is bee balm (*Monarda* spp.). They also love our California fuchsia and native honeysuckle [*Lonicera ciliosa*], which puts out flowers from June through August. And they like the penstemon, the cardinal flowers, the foxglove, the columbine. . . . We have 20 different plants, and they visit them all."

Rufous hummingbirds zip about the garden in spring and summer, while the Anna's stop by from spring through fall. The latter don't overwinter on the site, however, as the garden doesn't provide feeders. "The Anna's spend the winter in Seattle every year," says Jordan, "but almost always at feeders."

The presence of the Anna's hummingbird in the Pacific Northwest is a fairly recent development. As late as 1940, the Anna's range was limited to California and the Baja Peninsula. The area's balmy climate enabled the bird to forego migration, as it could always find flowers and insects on which to feed. But during the '50s and '60s, a vanguard of Anna's hummingbirds began to seek feeding grounds beyond their traditional range. Some shifted eastward into Arizona, while others drifted northward into Oregon, Washington and, eventually, British Columbia. Every year, a few plucky birds venture as far as Alaska, but they never stay. When one attempted to overwinter in the Alaskan town of Cordova, residents arranged to have it flown south on an Alaskan Airlines plane.

Biologists believe that a greater number of Anna's live in the Pacific Northwest than most people realize. In Oregon, the bird's population is larger and more stable along the coast, where the climate is milder; however, inland cities such as Portland, Salem and Corvallis each report at least four or five Anna's on their annual Christmas Bird Counts. In Seattle, as many as 24 Anna's have turned up on these winter tallies; the city of Victoria, Canada, on Vancouver Island has recorded 28.

Hummingbird researcher David Hutchinson believes these figures are probably low. "During a three-year study of the Anna's, I found that up to 100 live year-round in Seattle," he says. "The birds are also reasonably common in such cities as Tacoma, Bellingham and Victoria."

Hutchinson believes that the growth of suburbia has created new habitat for these opportunistic birds. "There are very few records of the Anna's in wild areas of the Pacific Northwest," he says. "They're almost all showing up in these nice backyards with feeders and ornamental plantings."

Most biologists agree that without the help of feeders, the Anna's attempt to colonize the area might well have failed, as the birds lack the instinct to migrate south in the fall. "I think in most winters, under most conditions, the Anna's is viable here," says Hutchinson. "But in really bad winters, feeders are probably crucial to their survival."

Seattle gardeners who attract Anna's hummingbirds note that the birds are largely dependent on insects and feeders in the winter months. Some ornamentals do, however, provide them with nectar. These include fall-bloomers such as hardy and bush fuchsia, cardinal flower, pineapple sage (*Salvia elegans*), impatiens, nasturtium (*Tropaeolum* spp.), snapdragon (*Antirrhinum majus*) and common witch hazel. Winter bloomers are scarcer but include *Camellia sasanqua*, viburnum, winter jasmine, rhododendron and the widely planted strawberry tree.

According to naturalist Penny Rose of Seattle's Discovery Park, the highly adaptable Anna's also visit wells drilled by sapsuckers. "I've seen them do this in winter," she says. "Sap has the same sugar content as nectar, and it attracts insects too, so the Anna's is probably feeding on the sap *and* the insects."

Ian McTaggart-Cowan, an internationally renowned biologist who lives in the flower-filled city of Victoria, British Columbia, says that Anna's hummingbirds have overwintered in his garden for the past 16 years. "There's always something in bloom here," he says. "Plus, there are lots of insects. You can look out at any time and see insects, little gnats and

Male Anna's Hummingbird

terested in the insects as the nectar," he says.

Another Victoria resident, Lyndis Davis, also welcomes both rufous and Anna's to her garden. She highly recommends hanging more than one feeder to help build their population. "I hang three, and it's really made a difference," she says. "Since I did that, I've had both rufous *and* Anna's nesting on my property. They've each laid claim to a different feeding station."

The hummingbirds in Davis's yard drink from a succession of blooming plants. In winter, the Anna's regularly visit a *Viburnum* 'Bodnantense' that begins to flower in fall and continues until April. They also feed from other winter-bloomers, including a flowering cherry (*Prunus autumnalis)*, a variety of heathers, Oregon grape and early-blooming white- and red-flowering currant.

Later in the year, they join the rufous in drinking from fuchsia, trumpet vine (*Campsis radicans*), shrimp plant (*Justicia brandegeana*), canary bird vine (*Tropaeolum peregrinum*) and honeysuckle.

While Davis enjoys watching the flashy little rufous in her garden, she takes even greater pleasure in the Anna's. "The Anna's seem to follow me around in the garden while I'm working, and they'll perch nearby and make their calls," she says. "I'm really quite fond of them."

Virginia Holmgren of Portland, Oregon also holds a special affection for the Anna's. The author of *The Way of the Hummingbird* and a longtime observer of the birds, Holmgren says that the Anna's have nested on her property for nearly three decades and remain with her throughout the year. "They showed up in my yard on August 9, 1968," she says, "and they've been here ever since—mothers, fathers, babies. They sometimes briefly move off, but they're never gone for more than a week or two."

While Portland winters are seldom severe, Holmgren says it does snow once or twice a year and ex-

so on—and you can see the Anna's up in the trees, going after them like flycatchers."

McTaggart-Cowan says that the Anna's nest in his yard in February, when the forsythia (*Forsythia* spp.) and witch hazel come into bloom. "Then later in the spring," he says, "the fuchsia and all sorts of things begin to flower. After that the hummingbirds get into the lilies and some of the azaleas."

McTaggart-Cowan says that both the rufous and the Anna's find plenty of red-flowering currant and salmonberry in the countryside, especially in lands cleared from logging operations. He has also observed the birds indulging on the blooms of wild Oregon grape (*Mahonia aquifolium*) and on a local currant (*Ribes lobbii*) that resembles a small fuchsia. "The *Ribes* attracts insects, and the hummingbirds are just as in-

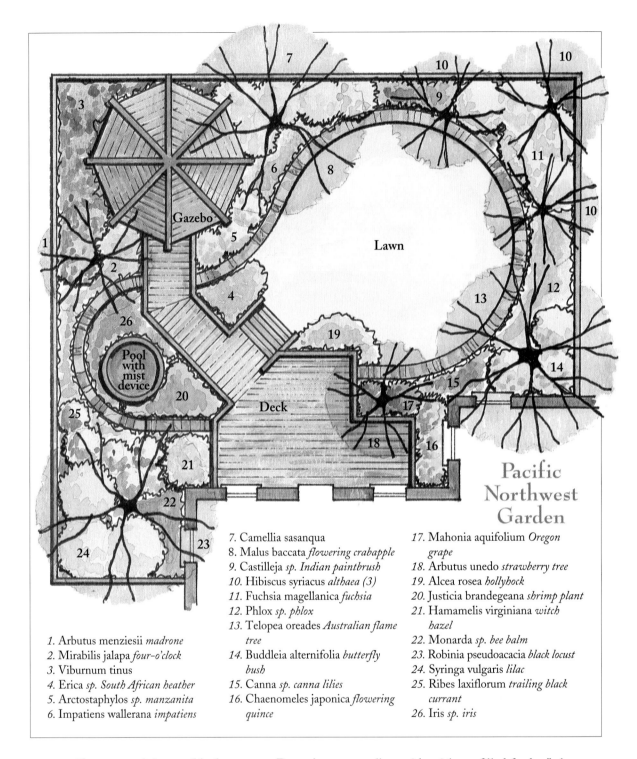

Pacific
Northwest
Garden

1. Arbutus menziesii *madrone*
2. Mirabilis jalapa *four-o'clock*
3. Viburnum tinus
4. Erica *sp. South African heather*
5. Arctostaphylos *sp. manzanita*
6. Impatiens wallerana *impatiens*

7. Camellia sasanqua
8. Malus baccata *flowering crabapple*
9. Castilleja *sp. Indian paintbrush*
10. Hibiscus syriacus *althaea (3)*
11. Fuchsia magellanica *fuchsia*
12. Phlox *sp. phlox*
13. Telopea oreades *Australian flame tree*
14. Buddleia alternifolia *butterfly bush*
15. Canna *sp. canna lilies*
16. Chaenomeles japonica *flowering quince*

17. Mahonia aquifolium *Oregon grape*
18. Arbutus unedo *strawberry tree*
19. Alcea rosea *hollyhock*
20. Justicia brandegeana *shrimp plant*
21. Hamamelis virginiana *witch hazel*
22. Monarda *sp. bee balm*
23. Robinia pseudoacacia *black locust*
24. Syringa vulgaris *lilac*
25. Ribes laxiflorum *trailing black currant*
26. Iris *sp. iris*

treme cold snaps may bring terrible sleet storms. During such spells, gardeners with an Anna's in their yard must take extra measures to prevent their sugar-water from freezing. Many rig up an electric light bulb to keep the feeder warm. Others keep several filled feeders inside the house and rotate them as needed, as Holmgren does.

"When it's cold like that, the Anna's will wait for me to walk outside with a refilled feeder," she says. "They'll even start to drink while I'm holding it in my hand, before I've had a chance to hang it."

Gardeners in other parts of the Pacific Northwest also have strategies for coping with cold snaps. Some wrap their feeders in a warm, woolen sock; others hang them under a heat lamp. According to hummingbird researcher David Hutchinson, during one bitter freeze in Seattle, people who kept their feeders lit all night had hummingbirds visit at midnight or two A.M.!

Ian McTaggart-Cowan of Victoria has also witnessed the Anna's feeding at night in frigid weather. "During cold spells, I'll get up when it's black-dark to hang out a feeder," he says. "As soon as I flip on the light and step outside, a hummingbird will be waiting.

"I don't know how they manage to do that, since they go into torpor at night. But the little rascal will somehow wake himself up out of torpor so he can have a drink of nice, warm syrup—sort of like having a cup of hot chocolate in the morning."

Although the Anna's most frequently overwinter at sites with feeders, they also seek out havens with winter-blooming flowers. One such place is Berry Botanical Garden in Portland, where the birds feed from the *Camellia sasanqua,* which bloom from December through January, and viburnum shrubs, which produce clusters of light pink flowers in early February. Other early bloomers include the 'Arthur Menzies' variety of Oregon grape and red-flowering currant.

At other times of the year, both the Anna's and the rufous regularly drink from the garden's fuchsia bushes, penstemon, California fuchsia, lilies, honeysuckle and native *Ipomopsis.* In spring and summer, it's not uncommon for visitors to witness a hummingbird courtship flight.

"They'll zoom high up into the air and then whiz down," says staff botanist Betsy Becker. "I've almost been buzzed myself when I've walked too close."

Farther to the north, those rufous hummingbirds that travel as far as Alaska arrive on the southeastern coast in early April. There, they zoom around stands of wild blueberry bushes. "We have four or five varieties of blueberries, and their flowers are out in early April," says Ketchikan resident Steve Heinl. "I always see the first hummingbirds on those."

Shortly afterward, an abundance of salmonberry bursts into bloom. In summer, other native favorites include Indian paintbrush (*Castilleja miniata*) and western columbine (*Aquilegia formosa*). Backyard feeders aid in attracting the hummingbirds as well.

Despite their tropical origins, rufous hummingbirds are surprisingly common along the Alaskan panhandle. Carolyn Parker, a botanist with the University of Alaska Museum, was amazed by the number she saw on a spring visit.

"I was walking along a road in southeastern Alaska and I saw all these rufous hummingbirds feeding on a bank of salmonberry," she recalls. "At first I thought they were bats because it was dusk and all these small, dark shapes were flitting by. But then I realized they were hummingbirds. I was easily seeing six or seven at a time, zipping by me and diving into the flowers."

Rufous hummingbirds usually nest as far west as Alaska's Prince William Sound, but they also turn up in Anchorage on an irregular basis. Dan Gibson, a biologist with the University of Alaska Museum, says that people suspect that a few rufous breed in that city, though a nest has never been found.

Perhaps more surprising are the dozen or so Anna's that lay claim to feeders on Alaska's southeast coast every fall. "The Anna's has a peculiar status here," says Gibson. "It occurs from fall to winter and it's *only* seen at hummingbird feeders. It's most numerous in the southeast but has shown up as far west as Anchorage and even Dillingham." Some coastal gardeners who maintain feeders attract the Anna's every year.

Gibson notes that, for such tiny creatures, hummingbirds are prodigious travelers. One rufous flew across the Pacific and ended up in Asia, landing en route on Russia's Big Diomede Island. An east-of-the-Rockies ruby-throat somehow made it to Nome, Alaska; another was found on the tundra at St. Michael's. And Costa's hummingbirds—considered desert-dwellers—have journeyed to southern Alaska on four separate recorded occasions.

"They're tough little birds," says Gibson. "I once saw an individual in dense fog on the Arctic coast of northwest Alaska. But before I was able to identify it, it was gone."

CHAPTER THREE

Chuparosa, Justicia californica

The Southwest

The mountain meadows of our Southwestern States
in midsummer, when their rich assortments of flowers
are in bloom, frequently swarm with humming birds of
a number of species feeding at the blossoms and pursu-
ing one another pugnaciously in pure exuberance of life.

Alexander Wetmore, 1932, National Geographic Magazine

EVERY SPRING AND SUMMER, nearly 2,000 hummingbird enthusiasts travel down back roads to Wally and Marion Paton's yard in Patagonia, Arizona. "Hummingbirders Welcome" reads a sign on the gate.
"Feeders Around Back." The Patons' feeding station is the only place
in the United States where the rare violet-crowned hummingbird is reliably seen.
As a result, their yard has become a standard stop for birders on southeast Arizona's
famous hummingbird trail. It joins the ranks of such long-standing hummer hot
spots as Madera Canyon, Ramsey Canyon and Drs. Walter and Sally Spofford's
yard in Portal, Arizona.

"People were out there blocking traffic trying to see the hummers as they
flew in," says Marion, "so finally we decided to open our yard to the public."

The mix of hummingbirds found among these hot spots is staggering. The

*Female Violet-crowned
Hummingbird on her nest*

usual assortment includes blue-throats, magnificents, broad-bills, broad-tails, black-chins, rufous, Anna's and violet-crowned (thanks to the Patons). Allen's, Costa's and the tiny calliope are also sometimes seen. In addition, species seldom seen in the United States wander across the border from Mexico. These glittering strays include the Lucifer, white-eared, berylline, cinnamon and plain-capped starthroat.

While southeast Arizona is undoubtedly the pre-mier hummingbird viewing spot in North America, the entire Southwest is rich in the flying jewels. From Phoenix to Tucson, from Albuquerque to El Paso, the tiny *picaflores* enliven courtyards and gardens, hovering before such plants as chuparosa (*Justicia californica*), ocotillo (*Fouquieria splendens*), penstemon, century plant (*Agave* spp.) and desert honeysuckle (*Anisacanthus thurberi*). They are as much a part of the landscape as the roadrunner and the saguaro cactus.

In some parts of the Southwest, gardeners enjoy the birds year-round, while in others they are regular backyard patrons from spring through fall.

If you garden in the Southwest, you probably already know that it's best to choose plants that require little water and are well adapted to the area's soil conditions and heat. Flowering natives perform superbly in most hummingbird gardens here, along with a few hardy imports—such as aloe and Cape honeysuckle—that have long blooming seasons. A trickling or misting water source can work magic as well.

As in other regions, a bank of feeders will help you attract hummers, but if you hang feeders, it is vitally important that you keep them clean. Sugar-water spoils quickly under the intense desert sun, especially in summer. To keep your backyard friends healthy, you may need to scrub and refill your feeders every day. (In winter, every three or four days will suffice.)

While gardeners throughout this region can achieve great success with hummingbirds, Arizona's hot spots should be experienced by every hummer fan.

These places attract more of the tiny birds in numbers and variety than any other place in the United States or Canada. So before we introduce you to some Southwestern gardeners, we'll set off on a quick tour of "Hummingbird Heaven," which is tucked in the lower right-hand corner of the Grand Canyon State.

Arizona's renowned hummingbird trail begins in Madera Canyon, which lies about 45 minutes south of Tucson. This well-watered canyon is tucked away in the Santa Rita mountains, one of several "sky islands" that tower above the Sonoran Desert. Each separate "island," a wildlife oasis, juts above the forbidding landscape. The hummingbirds, of course, home in on the bonanza of wildflowers strewn along canyon slopes. They also gnat for insects above the cascading creeks and seek nest sites in streamside trees.

Dave and Lyle Collister own and operate the Santa Rita Lodge in Madera Canyon. Clouds of hummingbirds are the lodge's main attraction, especially May through August, the peak hummer months. From dawn to dusk, the birds whir up to the

Male Broad-billed Hummingbird

lodge's feeders, which are clustered in a central viewing area and hung outside each cabin as well. The activity is most frenetic in the early morning and again as the light wanes, but is steady throughout the day.

The show is astonishing: a nonstop parade of iridescent broad-bills and black-chins, followed by a lesser number of magnificents, Anna's and rufous during migration. A smattering of other hummers make guest appearances as well. These range from the giant blue-throat to high-elevation broad-tails.

The Santa Rita Lodge's cabins are rustic but well recommended because of the birds. One visitor suggests a stay just to see the sunrise. "Even late risers should spend at least one early morning in Madera Canyon," she says. "The canyon faces north and the sun comes up over the east ridge. For the first 20 or 30 minutes, everything looks golden."

After the show in Madera Canyon, Wally and Marion Paton's yard is the next logical stop. Here, guests gather to watch such hummers as the elegant violet-crowned, as well as broad-bills, black-chins, rufous and Anna's crowd around a cluster of backyard feeders. Thrilling tropical strays such as the cinnamon and the berylline sometimes turn up as well.

During the peak season, hummingbirds chase and squabble with each other throughout the daylight hours in the Patons' yard. They make the rounds of garden flowers including penstemon, columbine (*Aquilegia* spp.), delphinium, autumn sage and four-o'clock (*Mirabilis jalapa*), and lap up five quarts of sugar-water a day. "We take our feeders in at night and refill them in the morning," Marion Paton says, "because the bats have found us." (Through much of the Southwest, nectar-drinking bats drain hummingbird feeders overnight. Some gardeners, like the Patons, take their feeders in at night to avoid this problem. Others don't mind the bats and simply replace the syrup every morning.)

The Patons' yard attracts a plethora of hummers because it backs up to Sonoita Creek, a lush riparian area largely protected by the Nature Conservancy. As with the sky islands, the habitat here presents a strik-

ing contrast to the Sonoran Desert. As you draw close to the Patons', you notice trees and greenery on the horizon. The air is humid, and you begin to see red-winged blackbirds instead of cactus wrens.

Ramsey Canyon, another Nature Conservancy property, is perhaps the most famous stop along southeast Arizona's hummingbird trail. One of its most prominent hummers is the nearly sparrow-sized blue-throat. In his classic volume, *Life Histories of North American Cuckoos, Goatsuckers, Hummingbirds and Their Allies*, biologist Arthur Cleveland Bent forever linked this bird with the canyon.

"The Arizona blue-throated hummingbird will always be associated in my mind with Ramsey Canyon," Bent wrote, "that interesting bird paradise on the eastern slope of the Huachuca Mountains in southeastern Arizona."

To study hummers, Bent traveled to the canyon with fellow biologist Frank C. Willard, where the two rented a cottage. "Here the stream ran almost under our cabin," Bent wrote, "and here we often heard the loud buzzing of the blue-throated hummingbird or heard its direct and rapid flight, as it whizzed by our doorway along the stream. It seemed never to wander far from the narrow confines of this mountain gorge and always seemed to feel perfectly at home and unafraid among the cottages and gardens."

More than half a century later, the blue-throat still patrols the cool mountain canyon, as do 13 other hummingbird species, from the equally large magnificent to the dainty calliope, which weighs no more than a dime. Preserve co-manager Sheri Williamson says that, during the summer months, black-chins and Anna's are the canyon's most numerous hummingbirds, with magnificents usually the third most common.

While all these birds are exciting enough, Mexican hummers with uniquely beautiful plumage sometimes appear—the white-eared, violet-crowned, berylline and Lucifer. On three occasions, beryllines have nested in the canyon, twice successfully. (To the delight of visitors, one female built her nest just outside the preserve's bookstore.) All this makes a trip to Bent's "bird paradise" a must on every hummingbirder's list.

The Nature Conservancy limits parking at the preserve to 14 cars at a time, which helps keep the flow of visitors to a manageable level. Inside the famous canyon, travelers gather on shaded benches to watch the dazzle of hummers at the sanctuary's feeders—up to eight species at a time, depending on the season. Six creekside cabins, each with a private garden and feeder, may be rented by guests as well.

The final stop on the hummingbird trail is the creekside yard of Drs. Walter and Sally Spofford, which is hidden down a side road in Portal. In this backyard oasis near the New Mexican border, guests sit on chairs and benches to watch a seemingly endless supply of hummers whirl around a bank of feeders. Black-chins and blue-throats are the major clients here, along with a mix of other Arizona regulars such as rufous and Anna's. In addition, the appearance of the rare, fork-tailed Lucifer sometimes sends a surge of excitement through the hummingbirders gathered to watch the show, as does the berylline.

Although all the hummers in this backyard preserve manage to drink from the feeders, the blue-throats definitely rule the roost. "They're like big guard dogs," says Nancy Newfield, who has visited several times. "I've seen them sit and wait for smaller hummingbirds to come in, and then swoop down and ride them out of view."

The Spoffords' feeders stay so busy with hummers that the couple refills them up to four times a day. When they leave town, they arrange for a sitter to do the job for them. The sitter feeds a roadrunner, too, as Connie Toops recounts in her book *Hummingbirds: Jewels in Flight*. During a summer visit, Toops' curiosity was piqued by a roadrunner that walked up to the Spoffords' patio door and tapped on the glass. "To my surprise," she wrote, "a young woman opened the door and tossed two chunks of beef to the bird."

The sitter explained that the roadrunner had been preying on the Spoffords' hummers. To prevent fur-ther losses, the couple decided to keep the bird fat and happy by feeding it chunks of meat.

An excellent way to round out a trip to southeast Arizona is with a leisurely stroll through the Arizona-Sonora Desert Museum near Tucson. Set in the rugged Sonoran Desert, the museum is part zoo and part botanical garden.

Though Gila monsters, elf owls and other desert animals live in this unusual zoo, hummingbirds are the stars. More than 20 of them fly freely within the museum's large, walk-through aviary: a shimmering array of Anna's, broad-billed, Costa's, black-chinned, broad-tailed, rufous, Lucifer and calliope. All are found in southeastern Arizona, though not necessarily around the Tucson area. A second aviary housing other desert birds is home to a single blue-throat. Head keeper Karen Krebbs says the blue-throat was too domineering to mix with the rest.

"He's two to three times larger than the others and he's quite aggressive," says Krebbs. "We've had to keep him apart."

The Arizona-Sonora Desert Museum is one of the few zoos in the world where North American hummingbirds have mated and raised their young. Krebbs attributes this success to the fact that the birds are quartered in an outdoor aviary open to sun, rain and heat. She also credits the *size* of the exhibit, which gives each bird enough space for a territory of its own. Keepers walk through the aviary at least once a day to observe the birds' activities.

When territorial problems arise, Krebbs sets up temporary lattices or adds new plants or feeders. "I try not to take an aggressive bird out of the exhibit unless I have to," she says. "I always try lattices and plants first."

Krebbs notes that because of the constant flow of visitors, the hummingbirds in the exhibit have become so accustomed to people that they show no fear. "They're very inquisitive," she says. "When people walk through the aviary wearing bright red clothes or a hat with artificial flowers, the hummers will fly right up to check them out. And when they're building their nests they're even bolder. They'll try to collect yarn from sweaters and if they see a loose thread they'll pull it off. They're especially attracted to sweaters and to old jeans with threads hanging out."

Because Krebbs has worked around the hummers since 1988, the birds recognize her. When she conducts a workshop in the aviary, they'll streak up and hover around her head. They even trust her with their young. Once, a Costa's nest fell apart when the hatchlings were five days old. Krebbs rescued the helpless babies and held them in her hand while an assistant built an artificial nest.

"When the female returned, she searched around for her young," says Krebbs. "When she finally found them in my hand, she calmly sat there and fed them!"

Krebbs hangs more than 30 feeders throughout the exhibit and also supplies the birds with fruit flies. The aviary's garden features more than 40 different kinds of nectar-laden plants, most of which are drought- and heat-tolerant.

Curator of Botany Mark Dimmitt designed the garden to provide the birds with flowers throughout the year. He cites ocotillo as the best overall hummer plant, both in the aviary and on the zoo grounds. He notes that the desert native performs well even in rugged conditions. It produces a profusion of flowers and is a very reliable bloomer. "At our elevation," says Dimmitt, "it blooms in April and lasts for three to five weeks."

Close behind ocotillo is chuparosa, a lower desert plant. "It flowers every year with great abundance," Dimmitt says. "We have colder temperatures at this elevation so it doesn't do as well here. But it's an excellent plant for lower elevations. It's a January bloomer here and the Costa's and the Anna's love it."

Other outstanding choices include shrimp plant (*Justicia brandegeana*) and Mexican honeysuckle (*Justicia spicigera*). "Shrimp plant will tolerate light frost and has a long blooming season of up to 10 months," he says. "Mexican honeysuckle is long-blooming too. Its flowers are a brilliant orange and they last from fall through spring." Dimmitt also recommends desert honeysuckle, though he notes that its blossoms are limited to a month in spring.

Another of the aviary's "very strong" hummingbird plants is western coral bean (*Erythrina flabelliformis*). "It's a brilliant plant in a desert landscape when it's in bloom," says Dimmitt. He notes, however, that it flowers in May for only a few weeks. Because of that limitation, gardeners may want to choose a coral bean hybrid (*E.* 'Bidwillii') instead; its blooming season stretches from March through October.

Dimmitt cites aloe plants as important food sources during the winter months. These nectar-filled succulents thrive in the Southwest's dry climate and have long blooming periods that extend from winter through spring. "The hummingbirds like them very much," says Dimmitt, "even though they come from Africa, where there are no hummingbirds."

Another first-class hummingbird plant is scarlet monkey flower (*Mimulus* spp.), which can bloom as early as late February and continue through May or early June. Dimmitt also suggests that gardeners try autumn (*Salvia greggii*) and Lemmon's sage (*Salvia lemmoni*), penstemon, scarlet betony (*Stachys coccinea*) and California fuchsia (*Zauschneria* spp.).

"*Zauschneria* is a super plant for the fall blooming season," Dimmitt says. "Both the riparian and the desert versions grow here. They are extremely profuse bloomers. They get going in September and last about two months."

In addition to flowering plants, the aviary features a number of trees and shrubs that provide the birds with shelter and perching spots. Some of these have broad leaves that the hummingbirds use as bathing platforms. Keeper Karen Krebbs says that the bathing tree of choice for most is the feather tree, whose large leaves resemble feathers. Staff members wet these lightly with a hose each day so the hummers can wash their plumage. "Their bodies are so light that they can bathe on those feathery leaves," says Krebbs.

On the northwest side of Tucson, Tohono Chul Park is an excellent place to view the radiant birds during the spring wildflower bloom. The park features striking desert landscaping with a number of known hummingbird attractors: Texas sage (*Salvia coccinea*), chuparosa, ocotillo, Baja fairy duster, ceniza (*Leucophyllum frutescens*), lantana (*Lantana* spp.), Mexican bird of paradise (*Caesalpinia pulcherrima*), hollyhock (*Alcea rosea*), canna (*Canna* spp.), red yucca, Wright's penstemon (*Penstemon wrightii*), California fuchsia and Texas olive (*Cordia boissieri*). The park's hummingbird garden, which brims with many of these plants plus tree tobacco (*Nicotiana glauca*), scarlet betony and Mexican honeysuckle, lies adjacent to a tea room. In spring, when many of the flowers are in bloom, the garden swarms with black-chins and Anna's. The tea room and its patio are favored spots for enjoying the show.

Hummingbird gardeners in the Phoenix area use many of the same plants to draw the birds to their yards. "A lot of us garden for hummingbirds," says Janet Witzeman, who is writing a book on county birds. "This is a great place for hummers because you can have them year-round."

The Anna's hummingbird remains throughout the year in Witzeman's garden, just as it does in many Arizona yards. The range of this handsome hummer was once restricted to California, but it has expanded northward and eastward over the past few decades. The Anna's began nesting in Arizona in the 1960s. Residents say that anyone who gardens for hummers will surely attract one of these cheeky little birds.

In addition to the Anna's, Costa's hummingbirds occasionally stay year-round in Phoenix-area gardens. The Costa's usually arrives in mid-October and leaves by the end of May. "They're winter-nesters," Witzeman says, "like the Anna's. They usually leave this

area in late spring, but some people with desert yards have them all summer."

The black-chinned hummingbird is also common in the greater Phoenix area. This close relative of the ruby-throat returns in March to raise its young and remains through the end of September.

The area's fourth hummingbird is the pugnacious rufous, which shows up in area gardens during its

Male Costa's Hummingbird with Penstemon, Penstemon *sp.*

southward migration. "A few come through in spring," says Witzeman, "but they're much more likely in fall. They're very common then, from July through September and especially in August. They just seem to take over."

Strays such as broad-bills, broad-tails and calliope hummingbirds are also sometimes recorded in the Phoenix area, though the four birds previously mentioned are the ones most gardeners can count on.

Because some hummingbirds live in Phoenix year-round, Witzeman has designed her garden to provide the birds with a continuous supply of nectar. "I have lots of shrimp plants," she says, "which the hummingbirds love. It's always in bloom. And I have some large bottlebrush [*Callistemon* spp.] that they really like too. It flowers almost all the time with bright red blooms."

Witzeman says that another long-blooming plant that the hummers target in her garden is Cape honeysuckle, a South African import with blazing orange trumpet-shaped flowers. She has a large one that has completely covered a wall. "It's a year-round bloomer," she says, "unless there's a frost. It dies during a frost but then comes right back."

In spring, chuparosa and a variety of penstemons produce nectar as well. In fact, Witzeman's garden offers so much natural food that she no longer hangs out feeders. "The hummingbirds come to the flowers all the time," she says, "all day long. I always see at least one or two hummingbirds when I walk into the yard."

In addition to flowering plants, Witzeman's garden features two water sources, a trickling waterfall near the front door and a pond in the back. "The waterfall has some little pools where the water drips down and the hummingbirds bathe there," she says. "But mostly we see them flying through the water, probably to catch insects."

One of Witzeman's co-authors, Bix Demery, lives at a higher elevation in Phoenix in a saguaro area. She describes her five-acre yard as a desert garden on the edge of a mountain preserve. Most of her hummingbird plants are drought-tolerant. The exceptions are Cape honeysuckle (*Tecomaria capensis*) and yellow bells (*Tecoma stans*), both of which require some additional water. "But both are long-blooming and the hummingbirds love them," she says.

Demery singles out chuparosa as a native plant that the birds especially like. "They're really attracted to those red, tubular blooms," she says. She also recommends other hardy natives like penstemon, desert willow (*Chilopsis linearis*) and ocotillo—dependable nectar sources that require no extra care—and notes that nonnative plants such as red yucca (*Hesperaloe*

parviflora) and aloe help draw the birds as well. "Hummingbirds *love* any of the aloes," Demery says. "I have a whole row of them, and the hummingbirds visit them all the time. They bloom on and off all year."

Four feeders in Demery's yard stay busy with hummers as well as other birds. Cactus wrens, flickers and Gila woodpeckers all belly up to the feeders, drinking them dry within a day. When this happens, the hummers perch nearby, waiting for a turn. Demery makes no attempt to chase off the invaders. Instead, she refills her feeders every day. She reasons that she should do so anyway in summer, when sugar-water can spoil in a single day.

Another Phoenix-area gardener is Eleanor Radke, who is collaborating with Witzeman and Demery on their book on county birds. She lives in the desert town of Cave Creek about 40 miles north of the city. Like Demery, she places chuparosa at the top of her list. "When that's in bloom, the hummingbirds desert my feeder," she says. "They really love those bright red flowers."

She also casts her vote for desert willow and tree tobacco, both of which bloom in spring. "The desert willow is found all along washes here, and the hummingbirds definitely like it," she says. "I have a hybridized version that's a darker pink than the native variety, and they really love that. They also like the yellow flowers on the tree tobacco."

To Radke's amazement, the hummingbirds also drink from the stately saguaro (*Carnegiea gigantea*). "The saguaro produce white, night-blooming flowers," she says, "that stay open for some hours in the morning. They bloom in May, and I was surprised to find that the hummingbirds use them a lot."

Radke suspects that Anna's and Costa's hummingbirds nest in her yard, as they treat her to their dive displays every year. She has yet to spot a nest in her garden, but recalls an Anna's that built one on a vine by the entrance to a building where she worked. "People walked past her all day long," Radke says, "and there she sat. She didn't seem at all concerned."

Like many other Arizona gardeners, Radke recommends the use of running water to attract hummers and other wildlife. Her yard features three shallow ponds connected by a series of waterfalls. These draw everything from hummingbirds to deer.

In Phoenix, the densely planted Desert Botanical Garden is an excellent place to watch hummingbirds and to take away ideas on how to attract them at home. Staff member Mary Irish says that on a walk through the garden, visitors can easily see at least a dozen hummers. "Our hummingbirds are very tolerant of people," she says. "They'll feed from flowers right along the path and pay no attention to people walking by."

Like any successful hummingbird garden, this Phoenix sanctuary provides the birds with an ample array of flowers throughout the year. During the winter months, its expansive aloe collection provides resident Anna's and Costa's hummingbirds with food. Other winter-blooming flowers include members of the *Lycium* genus, which are widely planted throughout the garden. "The Costa's are extremely fond of them," says Irish. "If you're in the natural desert here and find a *Lycium* you'll see a Costa's hummingbird."

Then, in early spring, waves of wildflowers brighten the garden. "A number of these are natives that the hummingbirds love," says Irish, "especially the penstemons." Irish singles out two of these profuse bloomers—Parry's and Eaton's—as extremely attractive to the birds. "Of course," she adds, "there is no penstemon that a hummingbird doesn't like."

Ocotillo and chuparosa also rank high on Irish's list. "The chuparosa blooms in winter here," she says, "and so does *Justicia ovata*." She also recommends Mexican honeysuckle, whose orange flowers thrive all summer long. Indeed, she notes that its blooms are so attractive to hummers that locals have dubbed it "hummingbird bush."

Irish says that a West Coast import, Baja fairy duster (*Calliandra californica*), works extremely well in local gardens. "That's a plant that the hummingbirds can hardly resist," she says. "We have three or four very large ones that bloom about 11 months of the year.

They're pretty much a permanent attractor. I have some at home, too, and I've never seen a day when there wasn't a hummingbird feeding on their blooms."

The flowers on saguaro and century plant attract hummers as well, along with other nectar-drinkers. "There are a lot of birds that just *cram* into the saguaro's blooms," Irish says, "from hummingbirds to doves, house finches and orioles. The same thing with agaves [century plants]," she adds. "Their flowers drown in nectar and all sorts of birds drink from them."

In addition to the lavish supply of blooms throughout the desert garden, a special bed was planted with an eye for hummingbirds. It includes such classic selections as scarlet betony, California fuchsia, cardinal flower, autumn sage and red yucca. Everything is labeled, making it easy for gardeners to carry ideas for plant combinations home.

Irish points out that almost all the plants in the garden are naturally rugged and require little water or extra attention. Exceptions include a few hummingbird favorites such as cardinal flower, which likes wet feet, and scarlet betony and autumn sage, which grow better in shade and a slightly rich soil.

Not only do the hummers work over the blooms in the botanical garden, but they fly into the greenhouse as well, especially when the Christmas cactus is blooming. A friendly little Anna's became so accustomed to feeding from plants in the garden shop that she began to collect her nesting materials there. "She'd fly in and look under the benches for cobwebs and bits of dead leaves," Irish recalls, "and then she'd rest for a minute on top of a cash register. She became so used to the greenhouse that if the door was closed she'd fly up and fuss until someone opened it for her!"

After her young had hatched, that same bird flew into the greenhouse to gather insects for her young from spider webs. "She just mined those webs," Irish says. "She would fly in and peck out all the bugs. I'm sure the spiders loved that."

Irish says that some of the garden's hummers become so tame that they follow her around as she works. She recalls a male Costa's hummingbird who liked to perch on the end of her watering wand. "Whenever I was watering the garden," Irish says, "he would fly up and sit on the end of the wand. He would jump into the water and then jump back to sit again. He was completely without fear."

At a higher elevation, hummingbirds whir about the plantings in the Boyce Thompson Southwestern Arboretum, which lies about 60 miles east of Phoenix. The arboretum is set in a natural Sonoran landscape dominated by towering saguaros, palo verde (*Caesalpinia pulcherrima*, or Mexican bird of paradise), jojoba, mesquite and ironwood trees.

Horticulturist Kim Stone says that while many plants in the garden attract hummingbirds, aloes put on the biggest show. "They're one of the very, very best," he says. "We have many different species throughout the arboretum and among them they bloom for months and months." He adds that the aloes flower reliably every year and can form huge masses 20 to 30 feet across.

Penstemons are also highly successful in the arboretum. Stone says that the four that really attract the birds are *Penstemon superbus*, Eaton's penstemon (*P. eatonii*), Parry's (*P. parryi*) and Arizona (*P. whippleanus*) penstemons.

He also highly recommends three plants in the *Justicia* family—chuparosa (*J. californica*), Mexican honeysuckle (*J. spicigera*) and red or ever-blooming justicia (*J. ovata*). "Chuparosa is our premier plant for hummingbirds," he says. "It's fast-growing and it flowers from early through late spring. We're almost too high for it here—we're at 2,000 feet—but you'll often see it in lower desert washes."

The arboretum also features a combination hummingbird/butterfly garden with a number of salvias. Of these, Stone singles out autumn sage (*Salvia greggii*) as the most appealing to hummers.

Rounding out Stone's list of the hummingbird "biggies" here are Baja fairy duster, which flowers throughout the growing season; eucalyptus, which provides food for the Anna's in winter; and ocotillo, which tolerates the harsh, dry conditions that other plants cannot.

The arboretum's hummingbird visitors include Anna's from fall through spring; Costa's and black-chins from spring through early summer; and occa-

Cardinal Flower, Lobelia cardinalis

sional rufous and broad-tails during migration. Broad-bills and magnificents are listed as rare.

Stone says that hummers are evident throughout the grounds, especially in areas with concentrations of flowers. Spring is the best time to visit, as the hummingbirds are most numerous then. Visitors during that season often witness their dramatic, high-speed courtship flights.

Stone notes that the arboretum's hummers become so tame that during the center's spring plant sale, they pore over flowers in the sales area. "They're pretty smart critters," he says. "We sell a lot of blooming plants and the hummers find them. While people are shopping for plants, the hummingbirds pleasantly fly all about, drinking nectar."

In nearby New Mexico, 14 different species of hummers have been recorded. Black-chins are by far the most common in most parts of the state, followed by broad-tails during spring and fall migration. At higher elevations, where they nest, broad-tails can also be amazingly abundant. Then from early July through October, rufous and calliope hummingbirds swing through during their leisurely southward migration. Unusual or rare hummers sometimes appear, including Mexican strays.

Due to this grand mix of birds, many residents have been inspired to plant hummingbird gardens and hang feeders. In addition, hundreds have volunteered to help with a hummingbird survey sponsored by the New Mexico Audubon Council, Randall Davey Audubon Center and Partners in Flight. Called the Hummingbird Connection, the study collects information on the birds' migrations, nesting behaviors and feeding preferences. Similar surveys have been launched—or continue—in Texas, Georgia, eastern Canada and the eastern United States. The state of Texas, with its flair for a catchy phrase, dubbed its program the Hummingbird Round-up.

Eleanor Wootten of Las Cruces, New Mexico, is coordinating the group's efforts. She notes that people from all over the state have signed up. Each participant receives a packet of wildflower seeds along with a survey form. In 1995, Wootten sent two kinds of penstemon. She notes that in her own garden, hummingbirds work over her penstemon beds all the time. In fact, the slender, tubular flowers are so popular with hummers that when the plants seed themselves between the bricks in Wootten's patio, she lets them grow.

Scarlet betony is another southwestern native that works like a charm on the birds. "I dearly love it," Wootten says, "and so do the hummers." Like many of the penstemons, betony reseeds itself.

Male Black-chinned Hummingbird

Wootten maintains three or four feeders from spring through fall. On several occasions an Anna's hummingbird has overwintered in her yard, leading her to keep up her feeders. Some of her neighbors have attracted both Anna's and rufous during the winter months.

Wootten says that the usual pattern for hummers in this part of the state is for black-chins to return in early April and remain to nest. Then broad-tails rocket through a little later. "We either hear the broad-tails or we see them, but they never stay," says Wootten. "They head on for the mountains."

After the broad-tails pass through, the black-chins remain as sole garden residents. This changes in early July, when the first of the southbound rufous appear. "The rufous stay until October or November," Wootten says, "though it's hard to tell which birds are which. I think some rufous are moving out while others are moving in." The calliope is also a fairly regular visitor in August.

Occasional strays further enliven the mix in area yards. Once, a female broad-billed, uncommon so far north, returned to Wootten's garden two summers in a row, arriving in June and remaining through August; and a blue-throat stopped off for a brief visit, also in August.

Wootten says that while she may count a dozen hummers at a time in her desert yard, New Mexican residents who live in the mountains or river valleys can attract hundreds, if not thousands, sometimes with feeders alone.

One such river valley is found at the Rio Grande Nature Center State Park near Albuquerque. There, black-chins are the most abundant hummers. Every year, they return to nest in the center's dense cottonwood *bosque* along the Rio Grande. Visitors often witness their soaring courtship flights in early May. "The black-chins are not at all shy when they're courting," says staff member Sondra Williamson. "I think it's because they're so intent on what they're doing."

In addition to natural nesting areas, the park features a demonstration native plant and herb garden with a section for hummingbirds. Among the plants there are autumn sage and several different penstemons; a feeder hangs as well. A second feeder attracts the birds to a backyard habitat area, while a third draws them to a pond lined with cattails and willows. "We hang that feeder on a swinging arm out over the water," says Williamson, "and the hummingbirds use it a lot. I think they know they're safe there—nothing can get to them."

Williamson adds that the black-chins probably nest along the water for that reason. They choose the trees that line the Rio Grande as well as those along the nearby Albuquerque Drain. "We have a bridge that crosses the drain," says Williamson, "and you can look out in the evening and see six or eight or ten hummers hawking for insects over the water."

Williamson says that in addition to nesting black-chins, broad-tailed and rufous hummingbirds sometimes visit the park during their late summer migration. The shy calliope is an uncommon guest as well.

While black-chins are the predominant hummingbird in Albuquerque, Santa Fe's higher elevation adds nesting broad-tails to the mix. The Randall Davey Audubon Center east of Santa Fe is an excellent place to see those hummingbirds. The sanctuary sits at 7,500 feet in the foothills of the Sangre de Cristo Mountains.

"When the broad-tails are back, *boy* are they back," says staff member Karen Copeland-Williams. "All day long, you can watch the males try *desperately* to attract a female. Every time you walk outside, they're out there doing their dive displays."

Copeland-Williams says the broad-tails generally return to the sanctuary in mid-April, as do the black-chins, which nest in the preserve's riparian areas. The new arrivals usually make a beeline for the sanctuary's fruit trees, which bloom in April and May, and for carpets of Indian paintbrush (*Castilleja* spp.). "They're very happy with the paintbrush," Copeland-Williams says. "It grows all over the place."

Later in the season, the hummers make the rounds of the many varieties of penstemon in the center's wildflower garden. The top performers there include Parry's and porch penstemon (*Penstemon strictus*), plus a third variety called *jamesii*. "The *jamesii* puts on a very good show with bright purple flowers," Copeland-Williams says, "and the hummingbirds love it. Plus, it's a long bloomer. Some penstemons quickly come and go, but that one seems to last all summer."

She also mentions that scarlet gilia (*Ipomopsis aggregata*) is a strong hummingbird plant in the wildflower garden. "That's real popular with the birds in late summer," she says.

As in many parts of the United States and Canada, Copeland-Williams reports that when the hummers first return, they are quite visible and highly

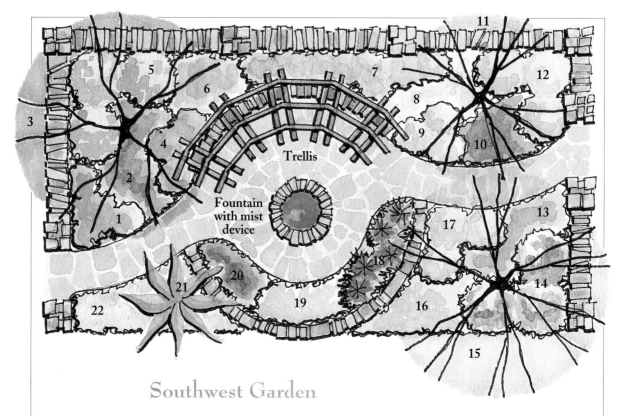

Southwest Garden

1. Chaenomeles speciosa *flowering quince*
2. Lobelia cardinalis *cardinal flower*
3. Erythrina 'Bidwillii' *coral tree*
4. Salvia leucantha *Mexican bush sage*
5. Cordia boissieri *Texas olive*
6. Anisacanthus thurberi *desert honeysuckle*
7. Asclepias tuberosa *butterfly milkweed*
8. Salvia lemmoni *Lemmon's sage*
9. Erythrina flabelliformis *western coral bean*
10. Penstemon spectabilis
11. Citrus *sp. citrus tree*
12. Justicia californica *chuparosa*
13. Fouquieria splendens *ocotillo*
14. Callistemon *sp. bottlebrush*
15. Chilopsis linearis *desert willow*
16. Justicia spicigera *Mexican honeysuckle*
17. Salvia leucantha *Mexican bush sage*
18. Hesperaloe parviflora *red yucca*
19. Salvia coccinea *Texas sage*
20. Justicia brandegeana *shrimp plant*
21. Agave *sp. century plant*
22. Lantana *sp. lantana*

active. But after the females nest, sightings can drop dramatically—sometimes to a single bird.

"A lot of people get frustrated because they don't understand what's going on," she says. "Well, during that time, the hummers are concentrating more on insects or they're busy defending their territories." She adds that, in spring, many migrants are simply passing through on their way to other nesting sites.

Following this lull, however, activity rebuilds to an even greater level. By mid-July, fledglings are out of the nest, adults are flying around and southbound migrants have joined the throngs.

Williamson notes that, during this frenzied period, the sanctuary's broad-tails and black-chins are joined by 10 or 15 rufous at a time and perhaps a calliope. The unruly rufous attempt to dominate the food supply, so there's a constant battle going on.

The hummingbird show in Texas matches that of its world-class wildflower blooms. Gardeners in El Paso and other southwestern towns report that their yards stay busy with the birds from spring through fall; some host winter strays as well. Although hummingbirds range throughout the area, one particularly good viewing spot is Big Bend National Park, that ruggedly beautiful natural preserve on the Texas Rio Grande. The park takes its name from the "big bend" that the river makes along its southern border.

Big Bend is big—in size and in hummingbirds. The park encompasses more than 800,000 majestic acres and three distinct habitats: the land in the Chihuahuan Desert, in the greener Chisos Mountains and along the Rio Grande. In spring, black-chinned hummingbirds and the rare Lucifer stream back into the park after spending the winter in Mexico. Ranger Mark Flippo says their return is fueled by two major blooms, that of the ocotillo and the tree tobacco, both of which are widespread in this part of Texas.

"Tree tobacco is probably the most important blooming plant in early spring," he says. "That's the one they visit the most. It's not native, but it's been naturalized. It's all over the place here, especially along river corridors. It starts blooming in February, earlier than anything else in the park, and continues on through April and into May."

Ocotillo, which is nearly as abundant, draws the hummers as well. At Big Bend, this hardy desert shrub begins to flower in spring and continues through the summer as long as there is rain.

Flippo says the black-chinned hummingbirds usually return in early March and begin to set up nesting territories along rivers, creeks or desert springs. During that time, they readily visit feeders and also rely on insects and tree tobacco. To start the hummer show, some campers hang out feeders as soon as they arrive at their sites. They often attract hummingbirds before they have their tents up!

In addition to these food sources, Flippo has noticed that the black-chins go after oak trees in early spring, when they start blooming. "I'll see them way up in the branches," he says, "though it's hard to tell whether they're gleaning nectar or insects."

The Lucifer hummingbird returns to Big Bend a few weeks after the black-chinned. This stunning, mostly Mexican hummer is the park's star: Big Bend is one of only two places in the United States where it nests. The other is in New Mexico's Peloncillo Mountains.

In early spring, the Lucifer mostly drinks from Harvard penstemon (*Penstemon harvardii*), ocotillo and tree tobacco. As the seasons progress, however, it zeroes in on a changing assortment of plants: desert willow, penstemon, mountain sage (*Salvia regla*), scarlet bouvardia (*Bouvardia ternifolia*), thistle, paintbrush and cardinal flower (*Lobelia cardinalis*). Its late summer favorite is giant century plant (*Agave* spp.), whose bright yellow blooms stand out in the desert landscape.

"All the hummingbirds really go after the agaves," says Flippo, "but the Lucifer in particular likes them." He notes that long-nosed bats are also attracted to their blooms, "so you can come to Big Bend and go bat-watching too."

Perhaps because both tree tobacco and century plant produce yellow blooms, Flippo has found that wearing a yellow bandana while hiking in Big Bend usually attracts curious hummers. Wearing red, though, works even better. Visitors who hike through Big Bend with red backpacks often report that the birds fly up to investigate the strangely shaped red "flowers."

The park hosts other hummers besides the nesting Lucifers and black-chins. This is particularly true during the summer rainy season, which begins in July and stretches into September, bringing a profusion of blooms, from penstemon to bouvardia to giant century plant. An insect crop also flourishes.

The park's Chisos Mountains rise dramatically above the surrounding desert floor. It is here that North America's two largest hummers, the blue-throat and the magnificent, reign. The blue-throat nests at higher elevations, while the magnificent wanders along the pine-clad slopes and may even breed there. Boot Canyon, a spring-fed hideaway within the range, is the best place to look for both these birds.

Big Bend also attracts broad-tailed hummingbirds, which nest in the Chisos, while the rufous migrate through in late summer. In addition, white-eared hummingbirds sometimes venture north from Mexico, further heightening the park's exotic appeal. Then, too, there is always the hope that other rare gems will appear—which is why the Southwest is known as a hummingbird paradise.

PART II

CHAPTER FOUR

Wild Columbine, Aquilegia canadensis

The Western Mountains

As we chanced, while hunting in the mountains, to pass through the haunts of this Hummer, it frequently happened that one of the little creatures, prompted apparently by curiosity, would approach close to us and remain poised in one spot, its wings vibrating so rapidly as to appear as a mere haze around the body; now and then it would shift from one side to another, its little black eyes sparkling as it eyed us intently.

Naturalist Robert Ridgway, 1877,
writing of the broad-tailed hummingbird

HIKERS IN THE ROCKY MOUNTAINS are often startled by the sight of a hummingbird hovering before them on a trail. The keen-eyed birds seem to shoot up out of nowhere to inspect a red bandana or a brightly colored backpack. "You'll suddenly hear this z-z-z-z and there they are," says Elly Jones of Montana.

No place in North America can match the sheer numbers of hummingbirds found in the western mountains. From the high meadows of the Canadian Rockies to the drier slopes of northern New Mexico, the tireless birds forage in patches of wildflowers such as Indian paintbrush (*Castilleja* spp.), penstemon and

Female Broad-tailed
Hummingbird at Penstemon,
Penstemon *sp.*

columbine (*Aquilegia* spp.). They also probe feeders throughout the region, sometimes in amazingly large throngs. In particularly good locations, *thousands* may converge at a bank of feeders. In such places, the thrum of their wings builds to a muffled roar.

"It's hard to describe what it's like to have so many hummers," says hummingbird bander Joan Day-Martin, who attracts such crowds to her backyard in northern New Mexico. "Sometimes I'll hear this loud roar that sounds like a jet taking off—but I'll look around and it will be the hummingbirds."

Hummingbirds are concentrated in the western mountains because the north-south ranges serve as natural highways. These majestic, flower-strewn thoroughfares lead up from Mexico, where many hummers spend the winter, to nesting grounds as distant as the Alaskan panhandle and the Canadian Rockies. After the nesting season has ended, the birds begin to stream back southward, following the mountain corridors to tropical climes. A substantial number of hummers also nest in the mountains, further adding to the activity.

Though all of North America's north-south ranges serve as major flyways for hummingbirds, by far the most heavily traveled are the southern and central Rockies. Every summer, the region pulses with the iridescent fliers, first with nesting broad-tails and later with rufous and calliope hummingbirds, which make a wide loop down through the Rockies during their fall migration. (In spring, the rufous and calliope bypass this flyway, navigating the mountain ranges of coastal California instead.) Black-chinned hummingbirds join the throng in drier locations, particularly on the western side of the Continental Divide.

Joan Day-Martin's home in Tijeras, New Mexico, lies near the southern end of this hummingbird highway at an elevation of 7,500 feet. Every spring, hundreds of broad-tails and a smaller number of black-chins show up at her feeders in late March or early April, at about the time that dwarf lousewort (*Pedicularis centranthera*), an abundant local wildflower, bursts into bloom. "As soon as that's out, they're here," she says, "although I hang my feeders sooner than that to catch any early migrants."

Day-Martin's five acres are naturally landscaped with piñon, juniper and scrub oak trees in addition to shrubs and wildflowers. She has added no additional plantings to this habitat, aside from some lilac bushes that have never bloomed. Instead, she supplements nature's bounty with a dozen carefully maintained feeders. These buzz with hundreds of hummers from April through June and build to 3,000 in July and August.

"By that point the air is just alive with hummingbirds," Day-Martin says. "They're everywhere you look. In fact, there are so many that the other birds in the yard will watch them as they eat. The black-headed grosbeaks in particular seem mesmerized."

Both broad-tailed and black-chinned hummingbirds nest in Day-Martin's yard. During the weeks when the females are busy with their young, Day-Martin scatters her feeders to break up any feeding territories and make it easier for the females to reach the sugar-water. After the young have fledged, she groups the feeders on her deck so that no hummingbird can protect them all.

By that time, migrating rufous and calliope hummingbirds, following the Rockies down from the north, have joined the multitudes in her yard. They begin to appear at her feeders in early July and remain through September or October. "By the end of October, I mostly have immature and female rufous," she says, "and then they leave as well."

Because of Day-Martin's location in northern New Mexico, she occasionally attracts stray southwestern hummers, including the magnificent, a hummingbird as large as a sparrow. "They pass through irregularly," she says, "usually after nesting season." Her rarest visitors were two white-ears—a male and a female—that wandered up from Mexico. They appeared in July and lingered for seven weeks.

Day-Martin believes that her feeding station attracts so many hummers because it lies on a major flyway. "I also think it has something to do with 'word of beak,'" she adds. "I think the word has spread that there's reliable feeding here."

Day-Martin's annual hummer extravaganza takes place in the mountains just east of Albuquerque. From there, the hummingbird highway continues north to the Colorado Rockies. As at Day-Martin's, broad-tails are by far the most dominant hummer. These high-mountain birds prefer to nest at elevations of 6,000 to 9,000 feet, usually in conifers along a creek. To the amazement of travelers, they readily mob feeders in small mountain towns, buzzing around these syrup sources like a cloud of bees.

Male broad-tails are the first to arrive in spring, followed a week or so later by the females. Because the males produce a loud trill with their wingtips, many gardeners have learned to listen for their arrival. The sound has been described as a metallic whine, a screeching buzz, a *Syrrr-syrrr* and even a bell-like ring.

Under the right conditions, the wing trill can be heard half a mile away. "Once in early April there was 30 inches of snow on the ground and it was 27 degrees and I *heard* a male broad-tailed," says naturalist Steve Bouricius. "I rushed out of the house with a feeder and held it in my hand as he fed."

"Once I get hundreds of them in my yard," he adds, "they sound like a cowbell chorus. There's an intense, ringing sound all around my cabin."

Horticulturist Mark Fleming of the Cheyenne Mountain Zoo in Colorado Springs decided to plant a hummingbird garden because he had heard so many broad-tails shooting overhead. "Whenever I wandered through the zoo, I'd hear the males but I rarely saw them," he says. "We're set in the mountains at 7,000 feet, and they were crossing overhead to feed on penstemon or clematis in the surrounding woods. I began to realize that this was a very rich area for hummingbirds, yet I was sure most visitors had no idea that they were here."

To lure the broad-tails down into the zoo, Fleming planted a hummingbird garden with more than 20 nectar-producers, from bee balm to trumpet honeysuckle (*Lonicera sempervirens*) to monkey flower. These bloom in succession from spring through fall. The garden also features three feeders, which are arranged in a triangle on the perimeter of the beds.

When the broad-tails return in early May, they are attracted to pink-blossomed beauty bush (*Kolkwitzia amabilis*) and red columbine. Then in mid-May, beds of Texas sage (*Salvia coccinea*), begin to blaze. Fleming reports that they "fight over that."

Fleming singles out pineleaf penstemon (*Penstemon pinifolius*), as another top plant in the zoo's hummingbird garden and also gives high marks to red-hot-poker (*Kniphofia uvaria*). "You can always see hummingbirds working over that plant," he says.

Among their preferred midsummer blooms are red lilies (*Lilium* spp.) and gay feather (*Liatris* spp.), followed by cardinal flower and fireweed (*Epilobium angustifolium*) in fall.

The zoo's hummingbird garden has proved so successful that it's not unusual to see 10 broad-tails at a time vying for the blossoms or staging their courtship flights over flower beds. "You can stand there and watch the males display," says Fleming. "They're completely unabashed."

As in most locations in the central Rockies, broad-tails are the zoo's most common hummingbird. They remain throughout nesting season, possibly raising their young in the blue spruce that flank the garden. Black-chins are the next most common. Like the broad-tails, they arrive in early May and remain to raise their young. Then in midsummer, rufous hummingbirds swing through during their southward migration, stopping off to replenish fat reserves. The dainty calliope, North America's smallest hummer, occasionally makes a brief midsummer appearance.

Hummingbirds are not quite as plentiful in the Denver area, which lies at a lower elevation than Colorado Springs and is more heavily developed. Still, gardeners have discovered that plants and feeders can draw dozens of the birds to their yards, especially during fall migration.

Wildlife consultant Tina Jones has pioneered this concept in the Denver area. Her backyard in suburban Littleton stays abuzz with the tiny fliers from spring to fall. Depending on the season, her customers include broad-tails, rufous, calliope and, once, two black-chins (which are very rare for the area).

"When I started out I thought I would get some hummingbirds, but not a lot," Jones says. "My goal was to have them stop in my yard during migration. That first year, I was totally flipped by how many hummers I got—eight to ten at a time, including the calliope, which is rare for the Denver area. Just two years later, I averaged 30 hummers at a time during fall migration—10 of which were calliopes."

Jones, a native plant specialist with a background in botany and ornithology, studied the foraging habits of hummingbirds in the wild before designing her garden. She noticed that as the hummers approached Denver they were mainly feeding on four plants: prairie delphinium (*Delphinium* sp.), prairie puccoon (*Lithos-*

Male Calliope
Hummingbird

permum multiflorum), wax currant (*Ribes cereum*) and snowberry bush (*Symphoricarpos albus*). She wisely added all four to her garden and then rounded out plantings with a profusion of other flowers.

"I try to have something in bloom from early April through the end of October," she says. "I mostly use plants that I've seen hummers visit in the wild, not only in Colorado but at other points on their migration route."

Jones designed her backyard to resemble a midgrass prairie. She uses dozens of Colorado natives in addition to plants from places like New Mexico, Arizona, Texas and the Dakotas. "My strategy is to have plants that the birds will recognize as they pass through," she says. Trees and shrubs provide the birds with cover and shady perching spots.

Jones says that she began gardening for hummers for ecological reasons. She strongly believes that habitat creation and preservation will help prevent a de-

cline in hummingbird numbers, as has already been documented with many songbirds. She notes that by feeding hummers, we can certainly help them, but she stresses that a healthy habitat—complete with plantings and cover—is even more critical to their survival.

Although Jones does use some nonnative blooms in her garden, such as Maltese-cross (*Lychnis chalcedonica*), she finds that native plants require less care. Most can better tolerate drought, heat and cold and seem more resistant to insects. "I let the bugs do their thing in my yard, and they seem to have reached a balance," she says. "And there have been unexpected benefits, like fireflies."

Jones has found that hummingbirds drink nectar from a surprising number of plants, but singles out two dozen as their absolute favorites in her garden. At the top of the list is skyrocket or scarlet gilia (*Ipomopsis aggregata*), which she grows in her midgrass prairie section. "My backyard is like a battlefield when that's in bloom," she says. "They go nuts over that."

Close behind the gilia is New Mexico native Mexican campion (*Silene laciniata*). It grows about 12 inches tall and shoots forth red tubular blooms. "The flowers must be very high in nectar," says Jones, "because that's a super big one in my yard."

She also highly recommends native penstemon, especially cardinal penstemon (*Penstemon cardinalis*), Rocky Mountain (*P. strictus*), scarlet bugler (*P. barbatus*), pineleaf penstemon, Eaton's (*P. eatonii*), and blue-mist (*P. virens*), all of which the hummingbirds fight over. She notes that blue-mist penstemon is an early bloomer that can help catch the eye of passing migrants. "I have about 30 of those plants in my front yard," she says. "They absolutely love it."

Another excellent hummingbird plant is butterfly larkspur (*Delphinium grandiflorum*), a nonnative that closely resembles Nelson's larkspur (*Delphinium nelsonii*) in color and size. "That's one of the main plants that the broad-tails feed on when they first return," Jones says. "It's been a real killer in my yard."

The birds also regularly feed from a native orange paintbrush (*Castilleja integra*), as well as from the wild four-o'clock (*Mirabilis multiflora*), which offers more nectar than cultivated varieties. The moisture-loving cardinal flower (*Lobelia cardinalis*), has also been a hit in her garden, and she says that California fuchsia, a late-summer bloomer, is "an absolute must."

Others in her top two dozen include double-bubble mint (*Agastache cana*) and giant hummingbird mint (*A. berberi*), gay feather, red-hot-poker, butterfly bush (*Buddleia alternifolia*), trumpet honeysuckle, bee balm (*Monarda* spp.), crocosmia (*Crocosmia* spp.), Texas sage and scarlet betony (*Stachys coccinea*). Surprisingly, purple coneflowers (*Echinacea* spp.) also draw the birds because they attract so many small insects. And, finally, Jones says the birds "go bonkers" over standing cypress (*Ipomopsis rubra*), which is native to Texas but grows well in Colorado and even survives winters. Supplementing this floral smorgasbord are six to eight feeders.

Jones has found that many of her most successful plants can be difficult to locate, and suggests that gardeners contact the National Wildflower Research Center in Austin, Texas for a list of local nurseries that carry native plants.

Although Jones has found that hummingbirds readily visit blue, orange, pink and even white flowers, their attraction to red is indisputable. She and her husband once owned a scarlet-red Chevy Suburban that immature birds in particular were always investigating. "They were *sure* it was a flower," she says. "They would fly up to the hood and stick their bill into the crack."

Another hummer enthusiast in Denver is Lisa Hutchins of the Denver Audubon Society, who gardens for the birds on a half-acre lot in Bow Mar, a southwestern suburb. Like Jones, she has arranged her garden so that some flowers are in bloom during spring migration, when the broad-tail zips through. But she times her biggest floral show for their southward migration, which in the Denver area begins in early July and stretches into October. During that time, she welcomes southbound broad-tails to her yard as well as migrating rufous and a few calliopes.

Hutchins explains that broad-tails once nested in Denver's riparian areas, though never in great numbers. (The city's altitude is 5,500 feet, while broad-tails generally prefer to nest at 6,000 feet or higher.) But the birds stopped nesting in the area in the 1950s, no doubt due to habitat loss.

"Right now, broad-tails come bombing through here in spring," she says, "but they don't stay long. They may take one sip at your feeder and then they're gone. They're in a hurry to get to the mountains and the best nesting areas." Hutchins hopes that if enough people plant hummingbird gardens in greater Denver the birds will start breeding in the area again. For now, though, she recommends that local gardeners focus their efforts on their southward migration.

"We start seeing the fall migrants shortly after the Fourth of July," she says, "and their behavior is much more leisurely than it is in spring. They may linger in your garden for a week or even two. Because of this, I find it best to concentrate on flowers that bloom at that time."

If Hutchins had to choose one plant to attract the birds during the fall migration, it would be cardinal penstemon, whose bright red blooms put on a show from mid- to late summer. "That's the best overall, a real biggie," she says. "The hummingbirds love it."

Also highly recommended is *Agastache cana*. "The hummingbirds really go nuts over that," says Hutchins. "Botanist Jim Knopf has given it the name double-bubble mint because it smells like bubble gum. It produces pinkish-purple blooms and does very well here. Mine can grow four feet tall."

Hutchins has found that pineleaf penstemon is also an excellent choice. During migration, she has seen broad-tailed, rufous and calliope hummingbirds drink from the pendant, scarlet blooms. This attractive, low-growing flower works well as a ground cover or a border plant.

California fuchsia (*Zauschneria* spp.) is another top pick for the Denver area. Hutchins recommends that people purchase them from a local nursery rather than by mail as they seem to do better that way.

The 'Gartenmeister Bonstedt' variety of true fuchsia, grown in hanging baskets, also does extremely well in Hutchins's garden. Other plants that hummingbirds frequent in her yard include red-hot-poker, cardinal flower, monarda, trumpet creeper (though she cautions that it can be invasive) and coral honeysuckle (*Lonicera sempervirens*). Of the latter, she especially recommends the 'Alabama Crimson' variety, whose rich color helps draw the birds in.

"Those are the biggies for hummingbirds here," she says. "For gardeners at higher elevations, another very good one is scarlet bugler. It grows wild and can be cultivated, too. It blooms in May and June when the broad-tails are nesting."

Hutchins arranges eight feeders at scattered locations in her garden, and has added a birdbath with a mister so the hummers can splash and bathe. She's been rewarded with a backyard show of up to 14 rufous and broad-tails at a time during fall migration.

"We occasionally get calliope and black-chins, too," she says of Denver-area gardeners, "but only if we're very lucky. For two years in a row, a male calliope has stopped off in my yard almost to the day. And I've had other calliopes, too, always during fall migration."

While broad-tails nest thinly at lower elevations, at higher altitudes they sometimes gather in phenomenal numbers. Peaceful Valley, Colorado, is one such spot. For more than a decade, naturalist Steve Bouricius has lived in a natural hummingbird garden in this remote mountain dale. He attracts the birds by the thousands simply by hanging feeders.

"It's quite a spectacle," says Bouricius. "Even in the hot spots in Arizona, I've never seen anything *close* to the gatherings around my cabin. It's hard to estimate numbers, but at peak times I probably attract 3,000 or more a day."

Bouricius's cabin sits at an elevation of 8,525 feet, just yards from a river in a vast, unbroken forest dominated by spruce and fir. Native wildflowers are scattered throughout the area, particularly on south-facing slopes. The hummingbirds set up territories around these food sources and also pay visits to Bouricius's 30 feeders, which he hangs in clusters around the cabin. Insects provide needed calories as well.

"The females eat more insects than the males and tend to stay along the river," says Bouricius. "During nesting season, you can easily see a dozen or more females catching gnats above the water."

Peaceful Valley lies about 20 miles west of Lyons, Colorado, in a secluded mountain valley. Bouricius says that broad-tails begin to return to the area in mid- to late April. By the second week of May, whole squadrons are back.

"I put out one or two feeders at the beginning of April and gradually build up to thirty by midsummer," he says. "I've found that they return as early as April 17 and will come to locations where I've had feeders before."

Female broad-tails begin to appear shortly after the first males. "Once the females arrive, the males will be out there doing their courtship displays. I see dive displays constantly throughout the yard, throughout the day. I think some of them practice their dives even before the females are back. Then, once the females return, they start doing their shuttle displays."

By June 20, Bouricius says that his yard is really active. "There can be hundreds of males flying around the cabin," he says. "By the peak of the season, they go through six gallons of sugar-water a day."

While the males aggressively defend their territories, the females busy themselves with constructing nests. Bouricius has watched the process many times. "You'll see them actively gathering nesting materials from the willow trees," he says, "as well as plant down from dandelions. They gather dandelion down at virtual hyper-speed."

Bouricius notices sexual segregation in the feeding areas once the hummingbird numbers build. "The males tend to take the more preferred, protected sites, while females are relegated to feeders in the more open areas. I'll find, for example, that the feeders in a small area may be used by one hundred or more females, while the males are mostly on the other side of the house, closer to the trees. It's fairly amazing when you get a lot of hummingbirds, how these differences show up."

By July, Bouricius has thousands of hummers in his yard, mainly broad-tails plus a surge of migrating rufous and a smattering of calliopes. "By that point they're shooting everywhere, all over the place," he says. "I'll have some feeders just full of hummers and others dominated by an aggressive male, with less dominant birds sneaking in and out for a drink."

At the prime feeding times in the morning and evening, however, even the dominant birds are forced to share. "At that point, you'll see 20 or 30 birds lined up at a single feeder," he says. So many hummers pile in to drink at dusk that visitors stop by to watch the performance. "The evening ritual here is to sit on the front porch to watch the hummingbirds," says Bouricius. "We invite friends over and school children, and

the hummers will come and perch on their fingers. It's quite a sight. You can put your hand around a feeder and have four or five or six birds land."

Bouricius attributes his success with the birds to his prime location as well as his dedication to scrupulously clean feeders. "I think if you live in this area, you could set up shop with 30 feeders and have success right away," he says. "One of the keys to attracting hummingbirds with feeders is to provide food *consistently* and to make sure that your feeders are very clean."

On the western side of the central Rockies, a drier, less mountainous habitat draws black-chinned hummingbirds to nesting sites in the Grand Valley. Coen Dexter attracts these striking birds—distinguished by a black and purple throat and a dark green back—to his home in Palisade, Colorado, which sits at an elevation of 5,000 feet.

The black-chins return every year in early April and remain to nest in the area. Migrating broad-tails also return at that time, but continue on to nesting sites at higher elevations. Then from early July through August, rufous, calliope and broad-tailed hummingbirds stop off in his yard during their southward migration.

"The rufous can arrive in the valley in great numbers during fall migration," says Dexter. "It's not uncommon to have a dozen or so around one feeder, and the black-chinned and the broad-tailed can get pretty thick. You always know when male broad-tails are at your feeders because you hear that loud metallic whine."

The diminutive calliope shows up in smaller numbers, but manages to hold its own in the crowds. "They feed lower down than the others," says Dexter. "I've noticed that in my yard, they especially like butterfly bush. They'll get down in that thick foliage where the others can't bother them."

Dexter singles out butterfly bush as the "single best plant" for the calliope. He has planted purple, blue and white varieties in his garden and the calliope visit them all. For all other hummers, he recommends trumpet creeper (*Campsis radicans*), whose

Male Rufous Hummingbird at Desert Four-o'clock, Mirabilis multiflora

showy flowers help draw the birds into the yard. "It's especially good if draped over a fence," he says, "so it really catches their eye."

Perching spots are important, too. In his neighborhood, the birds frequently sit in the widely planted globe willow (*Salix* sp.). He has noticed that they also work over those trees in spring, perhaps to glean insects or to drink sap from the stems of new leaves.

Dexter warns that anyone gardening for hummingbirds in the Grand Valley should watch for praying mantises, which lie in wait for birds as they visit feeders and flowers. Thousands of the predatory insects are released each year into the valley's peach, cherry, apricot and apple orchards. "They do help eradicate insects without spraying, but they present problems for hummingbirds," he says. "The mantises have spread all over the community. They're found in every yard."

To help reduce the problem, local hummer enthusiasts remove mantis egg cases from their yards and have learned to be selective about where they hang their feeders. "We try to avoid close contact with a bush where the mantises can hide," says Dexter. "And of course, if you see a mantis, they're easy to catch and remove. But it seems that for every one you remove there are two more to replace it."

While broad-tails are the most common hummingbird of the central Rockies, their breeding range ends in northern Wyoming. North of that point, the rufous and calliope are the dominant mountain hummers, while black-chins are most abundant in some locations. The reasons for these distribution patterns are unclear, though some scientists believe that altitude and weather conditions play a role.

Since the rufous and calliope travel north through California to their summer nesting grounds, many rufous and some calliope raise their young in the Pacific Northwest. Others loop eastward to the mountain slopes in the northern Rockies. After nesting, this easterly population continues down the

Rockies to Mexico, while others travel along the Cascades and the Sierra Nevadas. The rufous in particular can be quite numerous along those ranges during their southbound migration.

Western Montana can be equally exciting. At some locations, the calliope is the most abundant bird, while in others, the rufous or the black-chins dominate. Ornithologist Phil Wright of Missoula, Montana, says the calliope is the most common hummer in his yard, which is set on Rattlesnake Creek about three miles north of town. "We have some rufous here," he says, "but most nest a little farther to the north and at higher elevations." Black-chins visit his feeders on occasion, although they are far less numerous than the calliope or the rufous. Just three or four miles west of his home, however, the pattern changes and black-chins take over.

Hummingbird bander Elly Jones of Swan Lake, Montana, has concluded that the differences are due to the black-chin's meeker nature. "I've stared at habitat where black-chins are more prevalent and I can't figure out why they're there," she says. "I think it may be that the rufous are so tenacious that they lay claim to the best nesting sites. Then the black-chins move in to places where the rufous *aren't*."

Jones has banded hummingbirds since 1988. During the long Montana winter, when her garden is buried under snow, she prepares her minuscule bands and mends her nets. Then in mid-April, she begins to watch for hummingbirds.

"They usually show up here at about the same time that they do in Missoula, which is late April or early May," Jones says. "There's little in bloom, so they hawk for insects or zoom in to the feeders. But in '92 and '93," she hastens to add, "we had unusual weather. The wildflowers came in early, so the hummingbirds skipped the feeders and went straight to their preferred food. A lot of people around here worried that something had happened to them, but that's all it was."

Mountain wildflowers are so abundant that once they bloom, the hummers find no shortage of food.

"There are several different kinds of penstemon here, each found at different elevations and each with different blooming times," Jones says. "That's true of paintbrush, too. When I go hiking in the mountains, the paintbrush is absolutely breathtaking. The common variety at lower elevations is a scarlet-red with little tubular flowers. But at different locations they range from a deep, rosy red to almost purple and even yellow. In Glacier National Park you can hike and see whole meadows of paintbrush. It's absolutely spectacular."

Paintbrush blooms at lower elevations in mid-May. Next to flower is penstemon, followed by a wild honeysuckle (*Lonicera ciliosa*), which blooms through June and July. "That honeysuckle is everywhere," she says. "Its blooms are an orange-red, and the hummingbirds love it."

Then in midsummer, blazing stands of fireweed (*Epilobium angustifolium*) begin to flower and last for a month or so. "Fireweed is an excellent wildflower for hummingbirds," says Jones. "It's very common in clear-cut and logged areas—wherever there has been a disturbance. Of course, as you move up to higher elevations, the flowers are still coming on. If you go hiking, you see everything from spring to fall flowers, depending on the turns of the path."

The mountain wildflower blooms are so vast that the hummers tend to spread out across the acreage. But great concentrations of the birds can take place at feeders, Jones says, particularly in wilderness settings. She cites Ed Foss's home in the Swan Valley as a place where hundreds of the birds converge.

"The first time I visited, I was amazed," she says. "The whole place was just throbbing with hummingbirds. There was so much activity, you could hear their wings. You couldn't always see them because they were off in the vegetation, but you could hear them."

Foss lives on 200 acres that he has left completely natural, aside from a lawn and garden area close to the house. He maintains about 15 feeders which buzz with clouds of rufous and calliope hummingbirds during the summer months. Dozens of hanging fuchsia baskets provide food, as do native wildflowers.

"The activity stays like that all summer long," says Jones. "I used to put my net out on Foss's lawn and watch. I'd sit there, overlooking a pond, and have perfect views of hummingbirds hawking for insects."

At her own home on Swan Lake, Jones hangs four feeders on the shady side of her house. She also puts out hanging baskets of fuchsia and impatiens, which the birds regularly visit. Among her garden plants, she says their favorites include bee balm, coral bells, columbine, delphinium and wild honeysuckle. She experimented with red petunias, but reports that the hummers shunned them.

The addition of a small waterfall was successful. The top level is very shallow, with a thin layer of water that skims over a flat rock and then drops. "The water just wets the rock, and they'll sit down and splash there, even when it's cold," she says. "In fact, when it's just 29 degrees, I'll see them out there."

Jones's banding studies indicate that hummingbirds are loyal to nesting sites and migratory routes. She has had hummingbirds return to the same site, in the same week, five or six years after first being banded. She has also helped confirm that the birds follow the mountains during their journey south. In 1994, Jones banded a rufous at Swan Lake. Eight days later, longtime hummingbird bander William Calder, professor of Ecology and Evolutionary Biology at the University of Arizona, Tucson, captured the bird at his mountain banding site in Gothic, Colorado.

Jones recommends that visitors to Montana watch for hummingbirds in Glacier National Park and the Jewel Basin Hiking Area just east of Big Fork, especially in July and early August. "You couldn't design a prettier landscape than Jewel Basin," she says. "Flowers grow out of rocks that form natural steps, and there are tiny, trickling waterfalls." Like others familiar with the mountains, she advises hikers to wear something red to catch a hummer's eye.

Both rufous and calliope hummingbirds nest in the Canadian Rockies, which lie a little farther to the north. The hovering birds are a common sight at feeders in mountain towns such as Waterton Park, Banff and Jasper. Little gardening is done to attract them, however, as the deer and elk tend to eat everything in sight. Many hummingbird enthusiasts circumvent these browsers by hanging flower baskets out of their reach. Others have discovered that native plants, including columbine and fireweed, hold little attraction for deer and elk.

Roy Richards of Jasper, Alberta, is an avid birder who frequently hikes in Jasper National Park. He says that both rufous and calliope hummingbirds return to the Canadian Rockies in mid-May and depart by late August or early September. Early arrivals find little on which to feed other than insects. Soon afterward, however, thickets of chokecherry bushes (*Prunus virginiana*) begin to bloom, followed by a full procession of mountain wildflowers.

Richards says there are a large number of rufous hummingbirds in the northern Rockies. Many of them breed in the Mount Robson area, where they build their nests on the downturned branches of conifer trees. They nest in mountain towns as well, often choosing large fir trees. Every year they stage their mating displays in Richards's yard.

Calliope hummingbirds find more secluded nesting sites. Richards has yet to discover one of their nests, yet he knows where to find the birds. He most often spots them in swampy areas or perched in an alder or willow tree overhanging water.

"In fact, I know of two perching spots where I can always see a calliope," he says. "Both are branches that extend over a pond and offer a good view. You can always see a calliope sitting there, looking around. They'll go off and feed and then come back and sit again."

Hummer enthusiasts who have their feeders ready and waiting easily attract both species. The birds are thickest at feeders in spring, but soon scatter to nest throughout the region. After the young have fledged, they return in force to backyards.

"We usually see our first hummingbirds at feeders because there's not much available in the wild," says naturalist Janice Smith of Waterton Lakes Na-

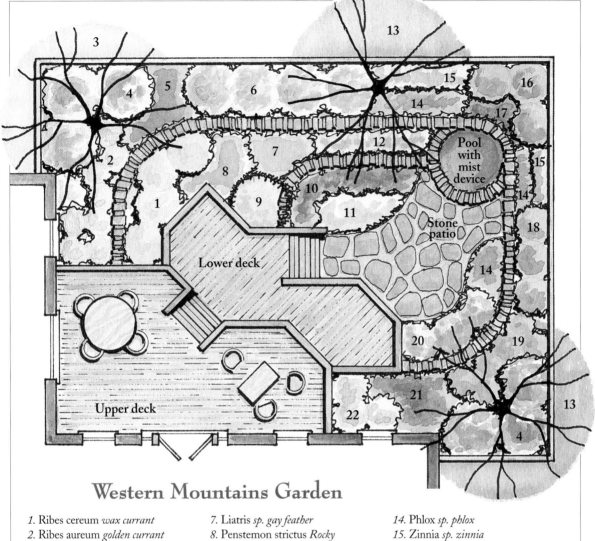

Western Mountains Garden

1. Ribes cereum *wax currant*
2. Ribes aureum *golden currant*
3. Aesculus hippocastanum *horsechestnut*
4. Buddleia alternifolia *butterfly bush*
5. Mirabilis multiflora *desert four-o'clock*
6. Cephalanthus occidentalis *buttonbush*
7. Liatris *sp. gay feather*
8. Penstemon strictus *Rocky Mountain penstemon*
9. Asclepias tuberosa *butterfly milkweed*
10. Salvia elegans *pineapple sage*
11. Impatiens wallerana *impatiens*
12. Salvia coccinea *Texas sage*
13. Liriodendron tulipifera *tulip tree*
14. Phlox *sp. phlox*
15. Zinnia *sp. zinnia*
16. Symphoricarpos albus *snowberry*
17. Salvia splendens *scarlet sage*
18. Zauschneria *sp. California fuchsia*
19. Salvia greggii *Rocky Mountain sage*
20. Monarda *sp. bee balm*
21. Lonicera ciliosa *orange honeysuckle*
22. Kolkwitzia amabilis *beauty bush*

tional Park. "They're always quite visible when they first arrive, especially when the males are doing their courtship displays. But then as the season wears on, they disperse to feed on wildflowers."

Smith often glimpses hummingbirds while hiking on mountain trails. She cites Indian paintbrush, which is "quite abundant" in the park, as one of their favorites. Later in the season, they forage from the blossoms of fireweed and various species of columbine. "We have yellow and blue varieties here," she says, "and they like them both." Penstemon is yet another mainstay. "We probably have six different species in the park," she adds, "usually in purple or blue." But Smith notes that she has seen the hummingbirds work over many different flowers, and not these top picks alone.

In late August, as the wildflowers fade from the Rockies, the hummingbirds vanish too. "At the end of the season, *boom*, they're gone," Smith says. "They just disappear."

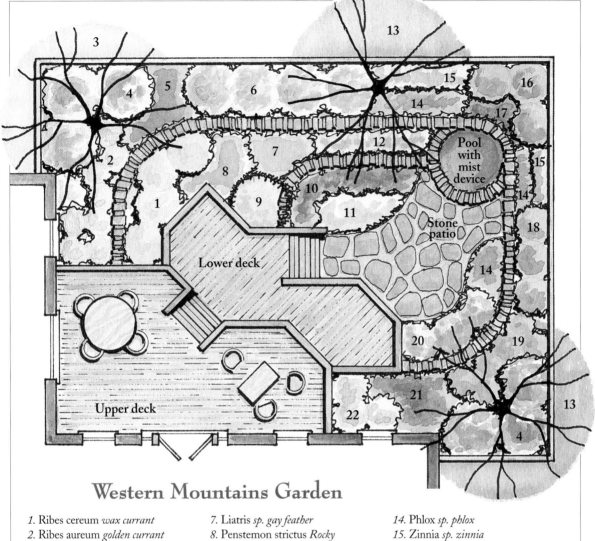

PART II

CHAPTER FIVE

Cardinal Flower, Lobelia cardinalis

The Southeast

In spring the ruby-throated hummingbird leaves its tropical or semitropical winter quarters and presses northward, keeping pace as the season advances with the opening of its favorite flowers. The bird's preference for some of these is so marked that it seems oftentimes to regulate its migration so as to arrive on the very day of their blossoming.

Winsor Marrett Tyler, 1936,
writing in Arthur Cleveland Bent's Life Histories of North
American Cuckoos, Goatsuckers, Hummingbirds and Their Allies

DURING THE PEAK OF FALL MIGRATION, some southeastern gardeners play host to as many as 400 ruby-throated hummingbirds at a time. One such lucky person is Olga Clifton, who lives just north of the Gulf Coast in Abita Springs, Louisiana. As you sit on her deck to watch the aerial acrobats streak about her spacious garden, you hear the *whrr, whrr, whrr* of hundreds of tiny wings.

Clifton's success in attracting the birds is partly due to location, for the ruby-throats tend to stack up along the Gulf Coast after funneling down from the north. Her one-acre lot catches their attention because it borders a woodland and is land-

Male Ruby-throated
Hummingbird at
Coral Bells,
Heuchera sanguinea

scaped with masses of flowers, including red salvia (*Salvia splendens*), shrimp plant (*Justicia brandegeana*) and the scarlet-flowered standing cypress (*Ipomopsis rubra*). To supplement these natural food sources, Clifton hangs as many as 38 feeders. In late summer, when local young have left the nest and more northerly-breeding migrants are passing through, the birds go through a 10-pound bag of sugar every two to three days.

Tremendous numbers of hummingbirds are not unusual in the Southeast, which sits squarely on the ruby-throat's migratory path. This dazzling little gypsy, distinguished by an emerald body and bright ruby throat, summers as far north as Canada and flies some 2,000 miles to overwinter in the tropical warmth of Mexico and Central America.

As waves of ruby-throats pass through this region, they stop to build up fat reserves on wildflowers and in local gardens before launching themselves on a non-stop, 500-mile flight across the often stormy Gulf of Mexico—one of the most amazing journeys in nature.

If you live in the Southeast, you can easily attract the migrants as they head toward the Gulf. Even if your space is limited to an apartment balcony, you can welcome the birds with a feeder, hanging baskets and potted plants. If you have a yard, you can create a ruby-throat paradise by hanging out extra feeders and including late summer- and fall-blooming plants in your landscape design. A single bed (4 by 12 feet) stocked with two plants each of Texas sage (*Salvia coccinea*), Mexican bush sage (*S. leucantha*), pineapple sage (*S. elegans*), anise sage (*S. guaranitica*) and Rocky Mountain sage (*S. greggii*) will produce thousands of nectar-filled flowers for the migrating birds.

Though ruby-throats, especially during migration, are by far the most numerous hummingbirds in this part of the United States, they are not the only ones. Two other species nest on the region's western edge and several others turn up during fall and winter. For this reason, many hummingbird gardeners here have two planting strategies: one for the ruby-throats, which arrive in spring and depart in the fall, and another for winter strays. Those who live along the coastal bend of Texas garden for buff-bellied and black-chinned hummingbirds as well.

Mexican cigar and flowering maple are two excellent choices for gardeners in this region. Both bloom almost year-round in the subtropical climate along the Gulf Coast and can easily withstand light freezes. If you live in a colder part of the South, where temperatures sometimes plunge below freezing, you can grow them in containers and move them inside during the winter months.

Mexican cigar (*Cuphea* spp.) is a Central American native and a classic hummingbird plant. When set in a sunny location, it produces dozens of tubular, reddish-orange blooms that look like slender cigars. Flowering maple (*Abutilon* spp.) is a scrubby shrub with maplelike leaves that has been long overlooked by area gardeners. It prefers part shade and produces a

profusion of delicate orange blossoms veined with red. Ruby-throats find the flowers irresistible, and for good reason: each contains as much as a thimbleful of nectar. (Although *Abutilon* hybrids are available in yellow, pink, salmon and red, hummingbirds seem to prefer the old-fashioned orange variety, *A. pictum*.)

Public and private gardens throughout the Southeast regularly attract significant numbers of ruby-throats during migration, and some locations become hummingbird "hot spots." At these places, hundreds upon hundreds of the birds converge. At first this may seem mysterious, since ruby-throats usually travel alone and along highly individual routes, a strategy that keeps them from draining the nectar supply. But these concentrations take place along natural landmarks, such as mountain ranges. Ruby-throats, like other birds, tend to follow such formations during migration, which explains why their flight paths may briefly flow together. Such gatherings often occur in mountainous regions, where an abundance of wildflowers provides the migrants with food.

Western North Carolina is one such hummingbird hot spot, particularly in such heavily forested counties as Jackson and Transylvania, which are situated at the meeting place of the southern Appalachian and the Blue Ridge Mountains. The area is a natural funneling spot for migrating ruby-throats, though many nest in the region as well. Ruby-throats are most visible in this area from midsummer to early fall, after the young have fledged and migrants have started to pass through. During that time, large numbers of ruby-throats whiz about flowers and feeders in the sparsely populated counties. The southbound hummers begin arriving in early July and reach their peak by mid-August.

"During migration, you can't sit in a chair for a minute without seeing a ruby-throat," says Jim Montheith of the High Hampton Inn, which overlooks 1,400 landscaped acres in the Jackson County town of Cashiers. "There are *tons* of hummingbirds—they're everywhere."

The High Hampton's grounds include expansive

flower beds where the ruby-throats feed. The birds also mob the large stands of jewelweed and other wildflowers that thrive along the inn's lake. In addition, staff members maintain six to eight feeders along a wide, wraparound porch furnished with rocking chairs. To the delight of guests, the little birds visit the feeders throughout the day, bringing a pleasant hum of activity to the mountainous setting.

In nearby Asheville, a demonstration hummingbird garden at the Western North Carolina Nature Center gives visitors ideas on what they can plant at home. Staff member Carlton Burke chose mostly native species when designing the garden. "We have cardinal flower (*Lobelia cardinalis*), jewelweed and bee balm (*Monarda* spp.) planted in large masses," he says. "Our garden is one big mass of color." Native trumpet creeper (*Campsis radicans*), columbine (*Aquilegia* spp.), rose-bay rhododendron (*Rhododendron catawbiense*), flame azalea (*Rhododendron carolinianum*) and butterfly bush (*Buddleia alternifolia*) round out the garden's plantings and offer additional nectar. Two feeders hung near trellises draped with coral honeysuckle (*Lonicera sempervirens*) provide an energy boost as well.

A second "hummingbird highway" crosses over middle Tennessee, on the western side of the southern Appalachians. Fran Vandenbroucke, a gardener who once lived in Sewanee, recalls that great clouds of ruby-throats would descend on the town in late summer, where they swarmed over the large patches of jewelweed growing in the moist soil along creekbeds.

"The birds routinely passed up cardinal flower, scarlet bee balm and trumpet creeper in favor of the jewelweed," she says. "In fact, in order to attract any hummers at all into my garden, I had to gather jewelweed seeds and plant them in a damp area at the edge of my property. Only then did they check out my feeders and flowers. But they still preferred the jewelweed, and it had to be the orange kind, not the yellow variety. And when I say clouds of hummingbirds, I mean that: hundreds of them, squeaking and twittering, and buzz-bombing unwary passersby."

Vandenbroucke later moved to Greensboro, North

Carolina, where she continued to garden for ruby-throats. Although she no longer lived along a major hummingbird flyway, at least a half-dozen migrants enlivened her garden during the spring and fall; and she always had at least one summer resident. "One summer I filled all my patio pots with impatiens and salvia and an aggressive male ruby-throat claimed it all as his," she recalls. "He used to attack me when I'd try to deadhead and tidy up the plants!"

The Ozark Mountains are a third hummingbird hot spot, particularly in forested areas. Planting strategies are similar to those elsewhere in the Southeast. As in western North Carolina, almost anyone who hangs a feeder will soon find their yard abuzz with hummingbirds. Those with well-designed gardens plus feeders can draw significant numbers.

Biologist Jan Self of the United States Forest Service comments that ruby-throats are so common in the Arkansas Ozarks that she sees them everywhere, even deep in the woods. "Many times I've been out in the forest and they've flown right up to me, particularly if I'm wearing a bright orange vest," she says. "They'll zoom up as if to say, 'What sort of flower are *you*?' They'll be out there working on the fire pink (*Silene virginica*) or the wild azaleas."

Self says the ruby-throats return to northern Arkansas as early as March and remain through the middle of September. "It's not unusual to have a swarm come through during spring or fall migration," she says. "I remember being out in my yard once and counting 20 ruby-throats around one feeder! I hang two feeders now. The hummingbirds drain them in a day during migration."

The Cliff House Inn, a motel, restaurant and gift shop on Scenic Highway 7, about six miles south of Jasper, Arkansas, is a popular place in the Ozarks for watching the ruby-throat show. Every year, from mid-April through mid-September, owners Neal and Karen Heath hang feeders outside the restaurant's 10 picture windows, which overlook a forested bluff known locally as "the Grand Canyon of the Ozarks." As diners watch, the busy little birds zip close to the

Hummingbirds like this male black-chinned often explore flowers that do not produce nectar, such as this Dianthus sp.

windows for drinks of sugar-water and then shoot off to chase each other.

"We get so many hummingbirds, they're kind of like bees, really," says Neal. "They're pretty thick."

After the ruby-throats have funneled down through such states as Virginia, Tennessee and Arkansas, they continue their beeline toward the Gulf of Mexico, feeding in gardens along the way. An excellent hummingbird viewing spot along this route is Callaway Gardens in Pine Mountain, Georgia. Throughout August and into early September, dozens of hummers at a time whirl about the center's Victory Garden, competing with native butterflies such as tiger and spicebush swallowtails. So inspiring is this sight that the garden regularly schedules workshops on how to attract the birds.

Naturalist LuAnn Craighton says that the ruby-throats especially like the garden's giant blue sage (*Salvia guaranitica*), cypress vine (*Ipomoea quamoclit*), coral honeysuckle, lantana (*Lantana* spp.), butterfly bush and giant turk's cap (*Malvaviscus arboreus* var.

mexicanus). "And they *adore* our pineapple sage," she adds. "They're always on that."

Another good viewing spot in Georgia is the Birdsong Nature Center in Thomasville, near the Florida border. A large "Bird Window" overlooks a garden set in the woods. As visitors watch, the ruby-throats streak up to drink from feeders and a succession of plants: red buckeye (*Aesculus pavia* var. *pavia*) and columbine (*Aquilegia canadensis*) in early spring and pagoda plant (*Clerodendrum speciosissimum*), a showy tropical perennial, in summer. They also visit a variety of flowers in the center's demonstration Butterfly/Hummingbird Garden, including coral bean, trumpet creeper, butterfly bush, pentas (*Pentas lanceolata*), coral honeysuckle and Mexican abelia (*Abelia floribunda*).

Birdsong Nature Center Director Kathleen Brady says that the ruby-throats zip about the garden during migration and breed in the area as well. "We usually have three or four males throughout the summer," she says, "and we know that females nest here. We've seen baby hummers being fed by their mothers while perched on trees near the window."

Bob and Martha Sargent, hummingbird banders who live in the countryside near Birmingham, Alabama, report that fall migrants begin streaking about their garden in early July. "We start hanging out surplus feeders around the Fourth," says Bob. "The male ruby-throats show up first and the females start to appear about 10 days later."

By mid-August, roughly 100 hummingbirds a day zip about their 10-acre property, flashing hot sparks of ruby and emerald when caught in full sun. Over the course of nine years of banding the migrants, the Sargents have discovered that many are repeat visitors, stopping off in their yard to rest and feed every spring and fall. (At least a half-dozen ruby-throats nest on their property, too.) Amazingly, some birds arrive on the exact same day every year. "You can only know that by banding," says Bob.

The Sargents attract the ruby-throats to their garden with lots of brightly colored, nectar-producing blossoms, from flowering maple to coral honeysuckle, shrimp plant, orange justicia (*Justicia spicigera*) and bouvardia (*Bouvardia ternifolia*). In addition, showy plants such as red bougainvillea, which provide little nectar, catch the migrants' attention as they wing overhead. ("The blossoms are so bright, they're like a beacon," says Martha.) In spring, more than 300 azalea bushes in shades of coral, delicate pink and pinkish red flash a signal to the hummingbirds, too.

Two ponds on the property, one with a recirculating pump, help produce insects for the birds. Other attractive garden features include feeders (up to 30 during migration), spaced six feet apart and hung in trees; a number of trees and shrubs for perching or nesting; and a deckside birdbath with a mist-sprayer where the hummers splash and bathe. "I can't overemphasize the importance of water," says Bob. "The ruby-throats love it."

The mister not only provides a place for the ruby-throats to cleanse their feathers, but it waters a shaded patch of jewelweed that thrives on the ground below.

"Jewelweed likes to have wet feet," says Bob. "We started out with three plants and within a year we had more than 300."

The Sargents note that when the jewelweed blooms, the ruby-throats feed almost exclusively on its nectar. After feasting, the hummers emerge coated with the sweet liquid. When that dries, they're left with white sugar crystals on their faces and caked on their bills. Sometimes their feathers stick up like a punk hairdo.

Ruby-throats are so fond of jewelweed that large masses of this wildflower almost guarantee clouds of hummingbirds during migration. Along the Natchez Trace Parkway in northern Alabama, an extensive jewelweed patch attracts hundreds of the chittering birds. The spot is known to locals, who bring their lounge chairs and a picnic lunch and sit and watch the hummingbirds.

In Mississippi and Louisiana, southward-bound ruby-throats begin arriving in mid-July and reach their peak by mid-September. Though that hummingbird delicacy, jewelweed, generally fails to thrive in the hot, humid coastal areas, gardeners have had great success with flaming beds of red salvia and Mexican bush sage, as well as with native plants such as trumpet creeper, red morning glory (*Ipomoea coccinea*), sultan's turban (*Malvaviscus arboreus* var. *drummondii*) and cardinal flower.

The wraparound porch of the historic Asphodel Inn near St. Francisville, Louisiana, is a relaxing place from which to watch the ruby-throat parade. At all hours of the day, hungry hummers whirl around the feeders that are spaced along the veranda. (The inn maintains six of these, which are refilled twice daily during the peak of fall migration.) Others seek nectar from the junglelike garlands of trumpet creeper cascading from the trees. Flowerpots and planters filled with showy impatiens also draw their attention.

A little earlier in the summer, when Asphodel's large mimosa tree (*Albizia julibrissin*) flowers, the ruby-throats congregate there, along with dozens of nectar-seeking butterflies. Owner Diane Smith says that during the peak of its bloom, the mimosa looks like "a decorated Christmas tree, with a hummingbird or butterfly on every limb." Bob and Martha Sargent also highly recommend mimosa, which not only produces nectar, but draws insects as well. Martha describes the tree as "a hummingbird supermarket—a one-stop shopping place for nectar and soft-bodied insects."

As the fall migration continues and more and more ruby-throats arrive at Asphodel, the little birds become increasingly bold. They fearlessly drink from porchside feeders and sometimes shoot within inches of guests dining *al fresco*. One year, a particularly spunky ruby-throat zoomed inside Asphodel's gift shop to "feed" on some silk begonias. After failing to find nectar, the bird attempted—without success— to find its way back outdoors. Finally Beth Smith, who was tending the shop, held out her index finger and the bird flew up and perched there. It remained there while Smith ferried it to the door.

Back in the 1820s, the artist John James Audubon completed 32 bird portraits for *The Birds of America* while living near Asphodel, where he tutored a plantation owner's daughter. It is heartening to note that the region—a peaceful place with pastures, woodlands and well-preserved plantation homes and gardens—is still a hummingbird haven. Oakley House, the plantation where the artist lived, is now open to the public as part of the Audubon State Commemorative Area. One of the birds that Audubon painted while in the area was the ruby-throated hummingbird, which he described as "a glittering fragment of the rainbow."

By the time the migrating ruby-throats have funneled down to the coast, some of the birds have already flown 1,500 miles. Still ahead is a hazardous 500-mile crossing over the Gulf of Mexico. The hummingbirds feed frenetically before attempting this final stretch, for they must increase their body weight by one-half or more, from about 3 grams to 4½ grams, in order to survive the 18-hour, nonstop flight. After storing up fat for the journey, the birds strike off from the coastlines of Alabama, Mississippi

and Louisiana. Substantial numbers also depart from the coastal bend of Texas.

While the ruby-throat migration creates hummingbird hot spots in mountainous areas, an even greater concentration takes place in Rockport-Fulton, Texas, located just north of Padre Island. Every fall, the vicinity becomes a staging area for the travel-weary birds. Thousands upon thousands of the migrants congregate in and around these two coastal communities to stoke up on nectar and sugar-water before attempting their journey across the Gulf. So amazing is the sight of so many hummingbirds that the town holds an annual Hummer/Bird Celebration to share the phenomenon with the world.

Though the ruby-throats begin arriving in Rockport-Fulton in late July, the celebration is held in mid-September to coincide with the peak of the migration. To the delight of festival-goers, as many as 200 hummers at a time vie for the feeders hung in local yards and gardens. Hundreds more riot around the wildflowers that seem to roll out welcome carpets across the surrounding countryside. These include a single trumpet creeper that smothers an entire farm building, as well as an abundance of wild sultan's turban and morning glory, all of which are ruby-throat favorites.

At the festival, a full slate of workshops and presentations focuses on hummingbirds and other natural history subjects, and field trips take visitors out to private gardens, where they meet hummer enthusiasts and watch the antics of the birds.

One garden is at the home of LaVerne and Fred Boden. Every year, the couple welcomes festival-goers to their carefully tended yard, which is filled with a profusion of nectar-producing plants such as sultan's turban, trumpet creeper, old-fashioned hibiscus (*Hibiscus rosa-sinensis*), orchid tree (*Bauhinia variegata*), shrimp plant, firebush, pentas and Cape honeysuckle (*Tecomaria capensis*). The Bodens also hang a dozen feeders, which they arrange in a bank just outside their screened-in porch. During the peak of migration, the feeders stay so busy that the Bodens refill them three times a day. Visitors are invited to pull up a chair and join the Bodens on their pleasant porch, which has an excellent view of the ruby-throats in their garden. They note that the hummers reach

Female Rufous Hummingbird

their greatest numbers in the early morning and late afternoon, though dozens buzz about the flowers and feeders at other times of the day.

"In the early mornings, ruby-throats pour into the yard," says the Bodens' son, Ron. "We easily see 200 at a time. There are so many hummingbirds, they don't bother to fight each other. You can walk into the garden and they'll whiz all around you. And if you're wearing a colorful hat, they'll land on that."

To help festival participants create a similar paradise at home, the town of Rockport has planted a Demonstration Hummingbird Garden in a roadside

park on Highway 35 North. The minisanctuary includes such hummer attractants as Mexican cigar plant, bottlebrush, firebush, shrimp plant, turk's cap (*Malvaviscus arboreus* var. *mexicanus*), Texas sage, Mexican bush sage and coral honeysuckle. During the festival, Nancy Newfield sets up a hummingbird banding station in the park. A limited number of visitors (25 per hour) are invited to watch her handle the birds. Each one is weighed, measured and banded—and then set free to continue on its southward journey.

A second mass migration of ruby-throats takes place in spring as the birds return to their summer nesting grounds. On rare occasions, coastal bird watchers may witness a hummingbird "fall out" after a storm. So exhausted are the birds from their desperate battle with wind and rain across 500 miles of open water that they pellet from the sky at the first sight of land. Many are so fatigued that they lack the energy to move when people approach them.

After Hurricane Andrew slammed into the Louisiana coast in the fall of 1992, many residents noticed a temporary surge in the ruby-throat population. Though an untold number of birds no doubt perished in the storm, the survivors were apparently blown miles inland. Steve Shurtz, a landscape architect in Baton Rouge, recalls an encounter with a dazed and exhausted hummingbird shortly after the hurricane's winds had died down.

"I was outside talking with a neighbor when I suddenly realized that a ruby-throat was sitting at a feeder less than a foot away," he says. "I thought it was strange that it didn't fly off, so I reached over and picked it up. It didn't seem at all concerned—in fact, it perched for a minute on my hand, curling its toes around one of my fingers. Then I placed it back on the feeder and it took a long drink. After two or three drinks of sugar-water, it finally flew off."

After that same hurricane, Donna McEnany of Baton Rouge also witnessed unusual behavior. Though none of the birds had approached her before the storm, afterward, when she stepped outside with a feeder, she was surprised to see eight or nine ruby-throats instantly fly up. The birds hovered in a cloud around the feeder, which was still in McEnany's hand, and took turns drinking as she walked across the yard to hang it. "I think they were so tired and hungry they overcame their fear," McEnany says.

Bob and Martha Sargent report that some ruby-throats have started resting on offshore oil rigs while crossing the Gulf. Many crew members feel so protective of the tiny birds that they maintain feeders for them during migration. One fall, a lone ruby-throat appeared on a drilling platform miles from the Mississippi coast. The bird was apparently too worn out to continue its southward flight, for it lingered on the rig even though the crew had nothing to feed it. Finally, the oil company dispatched a helicopter to ferry the bird back to shore. It spent the winter in a Mississippi gardener's greenhouse.

When the ruby-throats return in the spring, they rest briefly after their rigorous Gulf flight and then set about replenishing lost calories. Along the coast, they crowd into gardens with Japanese honeysuckle (*Lonicera japonica*), a plant introduced to this country during the 19th century. Interestingly, this is the ruby-throat's first choice in spring, though its fragrant white and yellow blooms don't share the "red, unscented" characteristics of most prime hummingbird

Male Buff-bellied Hummingbird at Shrimp Plant, Justicia brandegeana

flowers. The birds, however, have discovered that its blossoms are heavy with nectar. The migrating ruby-throats also feast on Cape honeysuckle, bottlebrush, impatiens, flowering maple and azalea. The first wave of the birds reaches the Gulf Coast in late February or early March; by early April they begin to appear in Tennessee and North Carolina.

In many areas of the Southeast, the ruby-throats time their arrival to the blooming of delphinium (*Delphinium* spp.), fire pink or red buckeye. Donna Legare, co-owner of Native Nurseries in Tallahassee, Florida, has observed the connection with red buckeye over years of hummingbird watching. "They must have co-evolved," she says. "People around here always see their first ruby-throat when the red buckeye blooms."

Though the ruby-throats migrate to nesting areas as far north as Canada, they breed throughout most of the Southeast as well. Many hummingbird gardeners enjoy at least one resident bird throughout the summer months, although those in urban areas usually find that the birds disappear for a month or so when they are off raising their young in surrounding woodlands. During this season, you should maintain enough feeders for the birds that remain and plant such hummer flowers as red salvia, pagoda plant (which the birds prefer to feeders), *Salvia* 'Purple Majesty', lantana, mimosa, coral honeysuckle, bee balm, bottlebrush and trumpet creeper.

Unlikely candidates such as zinnias are worth cultivating, too. Though they don't yield much nectar, hummers frequently test the colorful blooms. Zinnias also attract a tremendous number of insects, which supply the birds with vital protein and minerals.

The ruby-throat is not the only hummingbird to nest in the Southeast, though the region's two additional species have a limited range within the area. These are the black-chinned and the buff-bellied, both of which breed in coastal Texas. The buff-bellied is a large hummer with a red bill and green throat. It commonly feeds along streambeds and prefers a habitat with dense shrubs and flowering vines; good choices include coral honeysuckle, red morning glory and trumpet creeper. If you have a stream on your property, you can attract the bird by planting such vegetation along the banks. Despite its fondness for wild places, the buff-bellied is also a fearless visitor to backyard gardens. Many are drawn to shrimp plant, a flower they know from northern Mexico.

The black-chinned hummingbird is closely related to the ruby-throat and easily adapts to suburban life. It seems to recognize individual gardeners and will boldly whir up to drink nectar from a hand-held feeder. When seen in full sun, a band of brilliant purple feathers flashes below the male's black chin.

Southern Florida, like coastal Texas, offers a slightly different hummingbird picture from the rest of the Southeast. Because its climate is so balmy, with an abundance of flowers that bloom year-round, a number of ruby-throats overwinter there. Others pass through area gardens in fall as they travel southward. The tiny birds reappear in mid-March during their northward migration.

Due to Florida's proximity to the Caribbean, stray hummingbirds from nearby tropical islands sometimes show up in the southern part of the state. These include the purple-gorgeted Bahama woodstar, which occasionally wanders over to the Homestead and Lantana areas. The Cuban emerald, which is glittering green above and below, has been reported several times along the southeast coast as well as in the Tampa area. Adequate documentation of the Cuban emerald is needed, however, before ornithologists grant it a place on the Florida list.

Although gardeners in this region never attract large numbers of hummingbirds, they do spot them during spring and fall migration and sometimes attract overwintering birds. The best strategy is to make your garden stand out with a bold statement of red; you should also hang feeders. Once the hummers find you and you fill their needs—with nectar, insects and water—some may stay to enliven your flower beds.

Gardeners Ann and Phil Weinrich, who live in Lake Worth, Florida, along the southeastern coast, say that migrating ruby-throats most often feed on their Texas sage (*Salvia coccinea*) and their firebush (*Hamelia patens*), both of which bloom almost year-round. In other local gardens they have observed hummingbirds visiting the orange tubular flowers of the geiger tree (*Cordia sebestena*), the yellow blooms on necklace pod (*Sophora tomentosa*) and such flowers as pentas and lantana. Ann Weinrich notes that when a rufous overwintered in town, it spent most of its time on an orchid tree. Other excellent hummingbird plants for southern Florida include coral bean (*Erythrina herbacea*), trumpet creeper and coral honeysuckle.

Every winter, some unusual hummingbirds show up throughout the Southeast, sometimes lingering in local gardens for as long as four or five months. Hummingbird enthusiasts find these rare hummers just as thrilling as the ruby-throat migration. Because of this, many residents maintain their feeders year-round and design their gardens so that something is always in bloom. (The South's mild winters, particularly in coastal regions, make this possible.) When an unusual bird appears, an informal network of hummingbird watchers spreads the word.

The rufous hummingbird, a native of the Pacific Northwest, is one such stray. Every fall a significant number of the rust-colored birds wander as far east as Florida, blithely ignoring the migratory patterns of the species as a whole. (The rufous normally overwinters in Mexico.) These highly territorial birds begin to appear in southeastern gardens as early as August and remain in the region through late March.

The diminutive black-chinned hummingbird also wanders off course on a regular basis. Though the vast majority of black-chins migrate to the warmth of Mexico, a surprising number remain in the United States. Like the rufous, they may turn up in southern gardens as far east as Florida.

Every year for more than two decades, both rufous and black-chinned hummingbirds have spent the winter in Nancy Newfield's well-established garden in Metairie, Louisiana. The birds feed on various sages—pineapple sage, Mexican bush sage, Belize sage (*Salvia miniata*), *S. vanhouttii*—shrimp plant, turk's cap and other such reliable bloomers. Newfield also hangs as many as 15 feeders to ensure an adequate nectar supply.

On the rare occasions when the temperature plunges far below freezing in south Louisiana, Newfield increases her feeder solution to half-sugar, half-water to lower the freezing point. This is an emergency procedure and should not be used for more than two or three days, because the viscous syrup is more difficult for the birds to swallow. Other techniques to keep the feeder solution from freezing include wrapping the feeders with heating tape or hanging a light bulb nearby.

Though rufous and black-chinned hummingbirds are the most common winter strays in the Southeast, the buff-bellied, which usually migrates to Mexico, also appears on a regular basis. Even more thrilling are the Allen's, Anna's, calliope (North America's smallest hummingbird), broad-tailed, blue-throated, broad-billed and magnificent, all of which have shown up in southeastern yards within recent years. Even the occasional ruby-throat, which normally winters much farther south, has been reported. Reasons for this seemingly growing phenomenon are the subject of much debate. Some ornithologists believe that hummers are expanding their ranges because of global warming, while others suspect habitat destruction in the Tropics may be a factor.

Most hummingbird gardeners find it difficult to fill their yards with bold floral displays during the winter months. Instead, many rely on the red parts of feeders to attract stray hummers, and some have discovered that just about *anything* red will help lure the birds.

Before her recent move to another part of the city, gardener Miriam Davey of Baton Rouge, Louisiana, welcomed overwintering hummers to her partially wooded lot for more than a decade. Over the years, her garden served as a refuge for ruby-throats, black-chins, rufous and buff-bellies. Besides growing such hummingbird favorites as shrimp plant, pineapple sage and Belize sage during the winter months, she added extra color to her yard by tying bright red bows to bushes and trees. (Surveyor's tape is ideal for this.) Davey also maintained at least five feeders, evenly spaced around the yard, and hung out small mesh bags filled with rotten oranges or lemons to attract fruit flies, thus supplying the hummers with needed insects. Another clever hummingbirder solved the color problem by placing orange traffic pylons on his flat roof. Nancy Newfield took this a step further and painted her whole house red!

Should a winter visitor appear, contact your local chapter of the National Audubon Society so the bird can be identified and documented. And don't believe

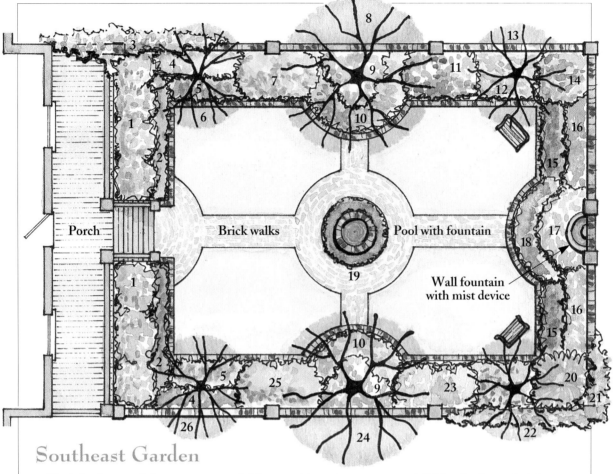

Southeast Garden

1. Rhododendron carolinianum *flame azalea*
2. Justicia brandegeana *shrimp plant*
3. Campsis radicans *trumpet creeper*
4. Chaenomeles japonica *flowering quince*
5. Pentas *sp. pentas*
6. Malus baccata *flowering crabapple*
7. Duranta repens *skyflower*
8. Albizia julibrissin *mimosa*
9. Ipomopsis rubra *standing cypress*
10. Salvia guaranitica *anise sage*
11. Buddleia alternifolia *butterfly bush*
12. Lantana *sp. lantana*
13. Hibiscus syriacus *althea*
14. Malvaviscus arboreus *var.* mexicanus *giant turk's cap*
15. Salvia elegans *pineapple sage*
16. Iris *sp. iris*
17. Hibiscus rosa-sinensis *Chinese hibiscus*
18 Mirabilis jalapa *four-o'clock*
19. Salvia splendens *red salvia*
20. Hedychium coccineum x coronarium *peach ginger*
21. Lonicera sempervirens *coral honeysuckle*
22. Camellia sasanqua
23. Weigela florida *cardinal shrub*
24. Eriobotrya japonica *loquat*
25. Cephalanthus occidentalis *buttonbush*
26. Erythrina 'Bidwillii' *coral tree*

the widespread myth that leaving up feeders in the fall will keep ruby-throats from migrating South. As Martha Sargent notes, the only way you can convince the birds to stay is to place them in a cage (which is illegal, of course, without a permit from the federal government). Biologists believe that the few ruby-throats that are found in winter are young birds that lack the fat reserves to successfully cross the Gulf.

If you live in the Southeast, you can enjoy the pleasures of hummingbird gardening in every season. In the spring and fall, your feeders and flowers will give migrating ruby-throats a needed sugar boost—and you'll benefit from watching their antics. In summer, the ruby-throats that nest in your yard will add life and beauty to your garden. And though overwintering hummingbirds are by no means assured, what could be more thrilling than to look out your kitchen window on a cold December day to see a shimmering West Coast hummer—hundreds of miles off course—hovering before your feeder on a blur of wings?

One such sighting and you'll be inspired to garden for hummingbirds throughout the year.

CHAPTER SIX

Male Ruby-throated Hummingbird

The East and the Midwest

"About nine o'clock one spring morning, when lilacs were in bloom, we discovered that the old lilac bush by the well was 'swarming' with hummingbirds—just come; we knew they were not there a few minutes before."

Jane L. Hine, writing in 1894 in The Auk, on the ruby-throated hummingbird

EVERY SPRING, Jo Houghton's country garden near Ithaca, New York, comes alive with ruby-throated hummingbirds when the lilac bushes (*Syringa vulgaris*) bloom. At least a dozen whirl about her feeders and plantings by the end of June. By late July, so many ruby-throats thicken the air that when Houghton walks out with a tray of feeders, they hover about her in a cloud. The boldest begin to drink while she's holding the tray in her hands.

The hardy little ruby-throat is the only hummingbird ordinarily found in the East and the Midwest, delighting gardeners with its glowing red throat, shimmering emerald body and ready acceptance of people. Every spring, it returns to nest and raise its young, bringing life and vitality to area gardens.

"The big excitement here is when the ruby-throats return," says Mary Brunker

*Male Ruby-throated
Hummingbird*

of Pequot Lakes, Minnesota. "From spring through Labor Day, they're darting everywhere—they're in the flowers, they're at the feeders, they're perched up in the trees."

The ruby-throated hummingbird overwinters as far south as Costa Rica. But as the days lengthen, it prepares for its northward migration by feasting on tropical flowers. After completing a perilous flight across the Gulf of Mexico, some of the birds remain in the Southeast to breed. Others continue on a northward journey that takes them well into Canada. They fan out as far west as Alberta and east to Nova Scotia. In the United States, the birds lay claim to nesting sites from Florida to the Dakotas.

In many parts of the East and the Midwest, the ruby-throat's arrival coincides with the bloom of such plants as lilac, flowering quince, autumn olive (*Elaeagnus umbellata*) or apple (*Malus pumila*) trees.

But the nectar supply is far from ample when the migrants first return, so the birds take advantage of the abundance of insects instead. Many also glean sap—and probably insects—from sapsucker drill holes. Biologists believe that these sap flows may provide the migrants with a vital food source in early spring.

While a migrating ruby-throat is able to survive on a diet of insects, sap and whatever wild nectar it can find, it is understandably drawn to a garden with a colorful display of flowers and feeders. If you live in this region, you can easily attract the birds by planting early-spring bloomers such as lilac or crabapple (*Malus* spp.) trees. (Though in some areas, even these lag behind the first arrivals.) You can add instant swatches of color by setting out hanging baskets or patio pots filled with bright flowers such as fuchsia (*Fuchsia* spp.) or impatiens. Should temperatures fall below freezing, the plants can be brought inside.

Your feeders, too, should be filled and waiting by the time the first ruby-throats appear. A good rule of thumb is to hang your feeders two weeks ahead of the birds' normal arrival date. That way, your food supply will be in place if the migration runs ahead of schedule. (Later on in this chapter, we will discuss normal arrival times for various parts of the East and the Midwest. You may also find it helpful to check with a local naturalist for specifics on your area, as well as to keep records of your own.)

Once the birds have discovered your yard, you can convince them to stay with a succession of plants that offer nectar throughout the summer and into the fall. You should also maintain your feeders and make sure that your garden provides an adequate number of trees and shrubs for perching or even nesting. Many gardeners have also found that ruby-throats respond to trickling or misting water, particularly on hot summer days.

If you live on New Jersey's Cape May Peninsula, for instance, you should hang your feeders by mid-April. Naturalist Pat Sutton says the ruby-throats usually return to her garden there near the end of April, just when the flowering quince (*Chaenomeles japonica*) begins to bloom. She notes that the bright, salmon-colored blossoms on her quince bushes help attract the birds, as do the five feeders strategically placed around her property.

"I'm a firm believer in using feeders in combination with flowers, in a garden free of pesticides," says Sutton, "especially a garden with trees, shrubs and vines so that cover and insects are available, too."

Even though Sutton's garden covers just half an acre, her yard "brims with ruby-throats" every year. A variety of hummingbird flowers add color to her garden from spring through fall, beginning with flowering quince and continuing with such summer and fall bloomers as bee balm (*Monarda* spp.) scarlet sage (*Salvia splendens*), Mexican sunflower (*Tithonia rotundifolia*) and butterfly bush (*Buddleia alternifolia*). Flowering shrubs, trees and vines—from lilacs to trumpet creeper (*Campsis radicans*) to tatarian honeysuckle (*Lonicera tatarica*) provide perching spots, insects and additional nectar.

Sutton says that a chain-link fence smothered with Japanese honeysuckle (*L. japonica*) becomes the hit of her garden in early summer (from about May 25 to June 15). During that time, the ruby-throats almost totally ignore her feeders and all other flowering plants, feasting instead on the vine's sweet nectar.

Sutton's garden is so well designed that ruby-throats raise their young on her property, frequently reusing the same nest. Once their young have fledged and migrants have started to pass through, the hummer population in Sutton's garden booms. "I have so many birds in late July and August that I have to refill the feeders every few days," she says.

In addition to being an avid hummingbird gardener, Sutton is a teacher and naturalist for the Cape May Bird Observatory, which is owned and operated by the New Jersey Audubon Society. Every August, she leads "hummingbird-watching" tours through Leaming's Run Gardens in nearby Swainton, a small town on the Cape May Peninsula. The gardens are well worth a stop for anyone with an interest in attracting hummingbirds.

Owned and designed by Jack Aprill, Leaming's Run consists of 25 flower gardens set within a woodland that features large American hollies, sweet gums, pines and other trees. Every year, Aprill and his staff plant more than 10,000 annuals in the gardens, including a long, serpentine row of two prime ruby-throat blooms—scarlet sage and cardinal flower (*Lobelia cardinalis*). So many hummers rest and feed in the gardens during the peak of fall migration that some have dubbed the site "The Hummingbird Capital of the East."

Sutton schedules her hummingbird-watching tours in the morning, before the gardens open, because the preserve is free of crowds then and the ruby-throats are more active. She begins each tour with a short talk on hummers and then leads participants on a walk through the grounds.

"The gardens are probably so good because Jack Aprill left much of the land natural," says Sutton. "He bought a forested area and planted these incredible gardens in openings in the woods. So not only do you see these beautiful gardens, but you walk through a breathtaking woodland that he's left undisturbed. His location on New Jersey's Cape May Peninsula also helps. Cape May is a natural funneling point for migrating birds."

Cape May experiences high concentrations of migrants, including hummers, because of its location. As the birds head southward through New Jersey, they reach Delaware Bay. Reluctant to strike out across miles of open water, they fly along the coastline, which points southeasterly, until they reach land's end at the tip of Cape May. There, they have no choice but to fly across the bay.

In Rhode Island, migrating ruby-throats reach Arthur and Ann Brown's woodland garden in late April. Not much is blooming then, so the Browns attract the birds with window boxes filled with red impatiens. "That works like magic on the ruby-throats," says Arthur. "It draws them right into our yard."

The Browns also hang four feeders, which they space throughout their garden so that one bird cannot dominate them all. They hang these in mid-April, just ahead of the ruby-throat migration, so that their feeders are in place before the birds arrive.

The Browns' property is ideal ruby-throat habitat. It sits deep in the woods, at the edge of a mile-long pond. In addition to the boxes of red impatiens set out on their deck, the Browns grow vivid stands of such hummingbird flowers as bee balm, salvia (*Salvia* spp.) and foxglove (*Digitalis* spp.). More red impatiens fill raised flower beds. The couple also plants cardinal flower in a damp area along the edge of a swamp. Ann says that the ruby-throats regularly drink from all those blooms, as well as from deep-red morning glories (*Ipomoea* spp.) twining along a fence. "They absolutely love those morning glories," she says. "They're on them all the time."

The ruby-throats also pay frequent visits to the tubular orange flowers of the trumpet creeper that covers a garden fence and to the flowers of the wild Japanese honeysuckle that has grown up along the back border of their yard. Then in late summer and early fall, dozens of the birds swarm over the large patches of jewelweed growing along the pond.

The Browns estimate that 15 to 20 ruby-throats remain on their property to nest and defend their territories throughout the summer months. After the young have fledged, their yard is filled with hummingbirds. The tiny birds generally remain at least through the end of August, but stragglers may hang around as late as October.

Like many gardeners in this region, the Browns take great pleasure in watching the emerald birds flash about their property. "We sit on the deck at dusk and it's hard to believe the noise," says Ann. "The hum of their little wings is just deafening. And they're so argumentative! You hear the steady '*chit, chit, chit*' of all their little voices. There's always a fight going on."

Ruby-throats, like all hummingbirds, vigorously guard their feeding territories by zooming after intruders with brazen courage. They only reach a truce when sheer numbers prevent any one bird from dominating the rest, such as during migration.

Jo Houghton and her husband, George, witness this phenomenon at their upstate New York home. The ruby-throat activity begins in their garden in mid-May, at about the time the lilacs bloom. Over the next few weeks, the population builds to more than a dozen birds, many of which stay to nest nearby. Then the population swells in late July and early August when the fledglings first appear. At that point, so many birds mob the feeders that they are forced to share.

"It's impossible to count them, but we have ruby-throats by the dozen in late July," says Jo. "This year I set up a video camera at the most popular feeder when the young were first out of the nest. There was a steady hum of activity for four whole hours. You could easily see 8, 10 or 12 ruby-throats at a time. At one point I moved the camera back and they looked like bees.

"I used to laugh at the idea of a feeder with three or four ports," she continues, "because I didn't think hummingbirds ever shared. But, now, if a feeder has six ports, it will have six birds and others hovering nearby. Even the mature males will drink from the same feeder as the other birds. I think what happens is that the young somehow overcome the territoriality of the males by sheer numbers."

The Houghtons' location plays a role in their phenomenal success with ruby-throats. Their two acres lie across the road from woodlands and are flanked by hedgerows. In their garden, lilacs, forsythia (*Forsythia* spp.), hollyhocks (*Alcea rosea*), bee balm, daylilies (*Hemerocallis*), cardinal flowers and jewelweed provide a succession of blooms for the birds. Trees and

Male Ruby-throated Hummingbird at Paintbrush, Castilleja *sp.*

mature shrubs offer shelter and nesting spots.

As ideal as this garden is, Jo says that only a few hummingbirds stopped off in their yard until she added feeders. She started off with one and has gradually built up to fourteen. The additional food greatly boosted the number of ruby-throats. Now the clientele grows each year as youngsters fledged nearby return the following spring to raise families of their own, and passing migrants spot the garden and streak down to check it out.

Jo and her husband find the antics of the ruby-throats highly entertaining, especially their insatiable curiosity. The young, in particular, investigate all bright colors: clothes hanging on the line, a shiny red car, autumn leaves, a colorful plastic bucket. They even try to drink from the red tops of feeders. "I think because their food sources change so much, they have to be curious and alert," says Jo.

Although the ruby-throats crowd around the Houghtons' feeders in early August, by midmonth they scatter across the surrounding countryside to feed on acres and acres of wild jewelweed. By the end of September, nearly all the ruby-throats have gone, headed for the warmth of Mexico and other tropical countries.

A little farther to the north, in Salisbury, Massachusetts, ruby-throats arrive in Carole and Gary Gura's garden in mid-May. Their intensively planted, half-acre property lies two miles from the coast and adjacent to a woodland. Every year, at least three or four ruby-throats spend the summer in their garden and raise their young there. Carole once found a nest when trimming some Canadian hemlocks; the down-filled cup was so small and well concealed that it resembled a knot on a limb.

Unlike the western Anna's hummingbird, which may build its nest near a door or a kitchen window, the ruby-throat is usually quite secretive when raising its young. The female frequently selects a site on a downturned twig overhanging a river or stream. She constructs the nest from plant down fastened together with spider webs. Then she camouflages the structure by adding bits of lichen to the sides. She often continues to add lichen after she has started to incubate the eggs.

Although it is difficult to find a ruby-throat nest, gardeners occasionally spot one in winter, when trees are bare. If you do happen to find one, be careful not to disturb it. The female sometimes returns to the same site year after year, giving you the chance to study the nesting cycle next season. (A telescope or binoculars will give you a closer view without disturbing the brood.) You may be lucky enough to see the female feed the nestlings—a startling sight as she inserts her long, sharp bill down each youngster's throat and pumps in a slurry of nectar and insects.

Although Carole and Gary Gura have yet to find an active ruby-throat nest, they consider the glamorous birds "the delight of the summer." The birds show up in the couple's garden every afternoon at about 3:30. So predictable is their return that the Guras invite friends over to watch the ruby-throat show.

"Their first stop is usually the feeder," says Carole, "and then they hit almost every flower in the garden. They visit the blueberry bushes (*Vaccinium* spp.), the buddleia, the pink and red impatiens, the blue lobelia (*Lobelia siphilitica*), the orange flame honeysuckle (*Lonicera* spp.), the clematis (*Clematis ligusticifolia*), the monkey flowers (*Mimulus* spp.). . . . The only plants I never see them on are those with double flowers like marigolds."

Farther to the north, an excellent viewing spot for hummingbirds is the Birds of Vermont Museum in Huntington. So many ruby-throats shoot by the front entrance that staff members joke about posting a sign that reads, "Warning! Hummingbird Crossing!" Every year, the glittering birds return in mid-May and remain through the middle of September.

Two feeders and outdoor gardens with flowering plants provide the birds with nectar, while nearby woodlands ensure a supply of insects. Former staff member Cinda Brown Bailey says the birds visit red columbine (*Aquilegia canadensis*) and a hanging basket of fuchsia in early spring. Then, as the summer progresses, they feed on hollyhock, followed by bee balm, cardinal flower and jewelweed.

A one-way observation window in the museum gives visitors a close-up view of the ruby-throats. A hummingbird garden planted outside the window draws the tiny birds in, as does a feeder hung near the glass. In addition, an outdoor microphone pipes in sounds, including the steady *thrum* of the ruby-throats' wings. "We usually turn the volume up so people can hear the hum," says Bailey. "They're always amazed by that."

Bailey says that after the young have fledged in late July or early August, the hummingbird activity reaches its peak. "It's very, very active then," she says. "I've counted six at a time—feeding, flying or perching—but it's hard to know how many there are. During August, we refill our feeders at least every two days." She notes that another excellent time to visit is early spring, when visitors sometimes witness the courtship flight of a ruby-throat male—daring aerial arcs performed at top speed.

In Chester, Vermont, Don and Nina Huffer welcome the ruby-throats in mid- to late May; the birds appear in their garden when the lilacs begin to bloom. Three or four remain throughout the summer and presumably nest nearby. "We've never found a nest, though," says Nina. "There are so many places where they could hide them."

The Huffers are forestry consultants who specialize in backyard habitat planning. Most of their 150-acre property is wooded, with about two acres close to the house planted with flower gardens, a vegetable garden, a wildflower garden and lilac bushes. The lilacs have staggered blooming periods, with some flowering early and others late. These, of course, help draw the birds to their yard.

Scarlet bee balm, blooming from late summer through fall, and native columbine (*Aquilegia* spp.) provide the ruby-throats with food. Summer-flowering plants such as phlox and the Huffers' carefully maintained feeders are also prime attractants.

Sap provides nutrients as well. On more than one occasion, Nina has seen ruby-throats drinking from the sap wells drilled by yellow-bellied sapsuckers, on trees close to the house as well as deep in the woods. "I find it fascinating that a hummingbird will fly that far into the woods," she says, "where there are no brightly colored flowers to attract them."

Betty Reckards of Rockwood, Maine, reports that *nothing* is blooming at her home on the Moose River when the ruby-throats arrive. "They usually return in mid-May when not a thing is blooming," she says. "There are insects then, of course, plus I hang feeders. I also put out hanging flower baskets."

Reckards knows that she attracts some of the same hummingbirds every year because if she's late hanging out feeders, the ruby-throats will check out the spots where the feeders *should* be. About two weeks after the first migrants arrive, Reckards' lilacs and a crabapple tree begin to bloom. She plants later-blooming morning glories and other hummingbird flowers for the birds as well.

Throughout the summer, at least two dozen ruby-throats hum about Reckards' riverside property. As a result, her gift shop on Route 15 has become a favorite stop for hummingbird enthusiasts. "People come back here year after year just to see the hummingbirds," Reckards says. "There are so many buzzing around that sometimes you're afraid that you'll be hit. Lots of times I've walked around the corner of the house and had one go whi-i-z-z, right past me. I've thought, 'Gee, if he ever stabs me with that beak . . .'"

The nearby woodlands and a thicket of bushes overhanging the Moose River provide the ruby-throats with secluded nesting sites. Reckards sees newly fledged young in her yard every year, but has yet to find a ruby-throat nest. "It's easy to tell which ones are babies because they are rounder than the adults and their bills are much shorter," she says. "And they make a little cheeping sound. I followed one of the cheeps once, and I found a baby hummingbird hidden in a bush, sitting on a seedpod."

Like other hummingbird watchers, Reckards has noticed that the fledglings seem confused the first few days. "They have a hard time finding the hole in the feeder," she says, "and in flowers as well. But once they figure out how to feed, they seem to mature quickly."

Even though ruby-throats overwinter as far south as Costa Rica, many of them nest well into Canada. Their total migration may cover a distance of more than 2,000 miles. In the province of Québec, they are common at feeders and flower gardens throughout the countryside. They may also be seen at such public gardens as the Montréal Botanical Garden and Les Jardins de Métis on the Gaspé Peninsula, especially during migration.

The ruby-throat's arrival in Québec seems timed to the bloom of lilac bushes and apple and crabapple trees. In the vast Montréal Botanical Garden, which covers 185 acres and is the second most important botanical garden in the world, the migrants stop off to drink nectar from the site's large collection of crabapple trees, as well as from the profusion of lilacs. According to staff ornithologist Corinne Tastayre, food and shelter are so abundant in the garden that some of the birds remain to nest there, even though ruby-throats seldom breed in urban areas.

"The garden is so big and has so many flowers that hummingbirds are there throughout the summer," Tastayre says. "You'll see the highest concentrations, though, during migration, from mid- to late May and again in late August."

Tastayre notes that hummingbirds are even more common in the countryside north of the city. "Out in the country, all summer long, you can see ruby-throats everywhere," she says. "They're extremely greedy. They visit both gardens and feeders. They especially like red tubular flowers, but they drink from many others as well."

Patricia Gallant of Les Jardins de Métis near the town of Sainte-Flavie on the Gaspé Peninsula says the ruby-throats return each spring when the crabapple trees send forth their pink blooms. Because the gardens are set at the junction of the St. Lawrence and the Métis River and are surrounded by woodlands, a number of hummingbirds nest there. They frequent garden blooms throughout the summer, but are most abundant from late July to mid-August, after the young have fledged. At that time, the gardens' Royal Walk becomes "a hive of activity" for the tiny birds, which twitter and chase each other above the generous borders of delphiniums. Interestingly, Gallant notes that the ruby-throats mostly ignore the two or three feeders hung near the information center, as so many flowers are available throughout the grounds.

Farther west, Sylvia and Jim Bashline of central Pennsylvania experience an even bigger ruby-throat show. They live in a wooded area in the Appalachian Mountains, where a profusion of trumpet creeper grows. As in many northern places, few flowers greet the ruby-throats when they arrive in early spring. Instead, they rely on insects and sap as well as the five feeders that the Bashlines provide.

"The ruby-throats usually return on May 1," says Sylvia. "The reason I'll know they're here is that one will come up to the window and hover as if to say, 'Well, here I am! Where are *you*? Where's my feeder?'"

Ruby-throats continue to arrive in the Bashlines' yard through the month of May. During that time, they consume about a cup of sugar-water every day. Activity is lower then, Sylvia says, because the birds are getting ready to nest and are setting up their territories.

Soon after the ruby-throats arrive, azaleas and then rhododendrons (*Rhododendron* spp.) bloom. Sylvia has seen them chase insects around both those plants. Then Japanese honeysuckle flowers in the woods, and phlox (*Phlox* spp.), bee balm, daylilies and other flowers offer nectar in the Bashlines' yard. That ruby-throat favorite, trumpet creeper, usually blooms in July and continues through the end of September; jewelweed also flowers at that time.

The hummingbird population on the Bashlines' property reaches its peak in July, after the young have fledged and the first of the southward-bound migrants are starting to pass through. By then, so many hummingbirds ricochet about the property that Sylvia can't count them. "I have no idea how many hummingbirds we have," says Sylvia, "but there are *lots*. We go through two or three quarts of juice a day during that peak time."

The Bashlines group their feeders fairly close to each other in front of a large picture window. Sylvia has found that by clustering them in this way, the feeding station stays so busy with hummers that a single male can't dominate them all.

The commotion is so spectacular that the Bashlines invite friends over to share the sight. They leave the windows open, to the further amazement of guests. "The noise is just overwhelming," says Sylvia, "with the hum of their wings and all that squeaking."

All this began 10 years ago with a single feeder. Since then, Sylvia and Jim have steadily increased the number of ruby-throats in their yard by adding additional feeders to accommodate more birds. Other factors in their success include the wooded setting, their location along a flyway and the abundance of trumpet creeper, jewelweed, phlox and other nectar-producing plants on their property.

Gardeners who live in more urban areas can en-

Female Ruby-throated Hummingbird at Lantana Flower

joy success with ruby-throats, though never in such numbers. In nearby University Park, Pennsylvania, for instance, wildlife biologist Margaret Brittingham attracts six to eight ruby-throats every year through a combination of feeders and flowers. In spring, she catches their eye with hanging baskets of fuchsia and geraniums (*Pelargonium* spp.) as well as two feeders. Brittingham also plants early-blooming bleeding heart (*Dicentra* spp.) and red columbine, followed by large stands of cardinal flower, which provide nectar in late summer and early fall.

Farther to the west, at the Cincinnati Zoo and Botanical Garden, exotic hummingbirds flash their colors in a hummingbird/butterfly aviary in Insect World. Visitors who stroll through this exhibit come upon such tropical species as the Peruvian sheartail, the rufous-tailed hummingbird and the oasis hummingbird. These birds seek nectar from flowers and feeders and zigzag after the fruit flies that staff members release. They also raid the butterfly feeders!

A similar exhibit at the Detroit Zoo, with tropical flowers and hummingbirds indoors and a demonstration hummingbird garden outdoors, has been extremely popular with the public. Zoo staff horticulturist Barry Burton is hopeful that the garden—which features successful hummingbird attractants like flowering Ohio buckeye (*Aesculus glabra*), bee balm, coral bells, red-hot-poker (*Kniphofia uvaria*), coral honeysuckle (*Lonicera sempervirens*) and cardinal flower—will inspire the thousands of area residents that see the exhibit to create similar habitats in their own yards.

Ruby-throats, of course, rarely nest in such populated areas as Cincinnati and Detroit, although they do pass through during spring and fall migration and sometimes enliven a single garden for two weeks at a time. These birds prefer to raise their young in more secluded sites, usually in a wooded area along a river or lake. For this reason, many summer cottagers have had great success in attracting hummingbirds. This is particularly true of those whose properties offer sheltering trees and overlook water.

Gardener Peggy Latimer is one such enthusiast. Every year, she eagerly awaits the return of the ruby-throats to her summer cottage on Ontario's Indian Lake. When the birds arrive in early May, they shoot around her three carefully spaced feeders and work over her large, self-seeding stands of bleeding heart, one of the few flowers in bloom at the time. Later, they feed from the succession of nectar-producing flowers on Latimer's deck, in her rock garden and along her woodland borders. Of the many flowers that they visit, Latimer notes that the birds' particular favorites include bee balm, impatiens, foxglove, coral bells (*Heuchera sanguinea*), delphinium (*Delphinium* spp.), nasturtium (*Tropaeolum* spp.), fuchsia and salvia. They also pay frequent visits to the wild columbine that grows on her property, as well as to the extensive patches of jewelweed along the lake.

Latimer deliberately leaves her property "rather wild," with pleasant splashes of wildflowers in addition to woodlands with native trees. This, combined with the property's lakeside location and its abundance of food, no doubt accounts for the fact that at least two ruby-throats nest there every year. Fledglings show up in Latimer's garden by late July, and in fall she sees "lots" of migrants.

One of Latimer's favorite experiences with hummingbirds was the time she chanced upon a female ruby-throat leaf bathing. Latimer watched the bird splash in the water collected on a large hosta leaf, which had folded up to form a small bathtub. The bather flicked her tail feathers and spread her wings on the leaf's wet surface. Then she flew off to preen in a nearby tree, stopping first to drink from a bed of impatiens.

Latimer's keen interest in hummingbirds led her to help coordinate the survey group The Hummertime Network. Based in Elgin, Ontario, the group collects data on ruby-throats from a cadre of feeder-watchers in the United States and Canada, and is actively seeking more volunteers.

In Minnesota, biologist Carroll Henderson, author of *Landscaping for Wildlife*, says that ruby-throats often zip around gardens in the Twin Cities area during spring and fall migration, though they don't nest there. "We get a burst of activity here in early May," he says, "but then they push on to nesting sites farther to the north. In the fall, we attract more, plus we have more plants to offer. In my yard, for example, which is in northern Minneapolis, I usually see three or four ruby-throats in May and two or three dozen in August and September. Many people in the Lake Country, however, get a spectacular show."

Henderson notes that few flowers are in bloom when the ruby-throats return to the state. "Columbine is one early-spring plant," he says, "and people who put fuchsia baskets on their decks see them go to that."

In summer and fall, however, gardeners can attract the birds with a variety of plants. "One very good one is scarlet runner bean, which you can train to climb up a fence or trellis," says Henderson. "Cardinal flowers also work particularly well, and bee balm, especially the mildew-resistant 'Garden View' variety."

Also high on his list are hostas (*Hosta* spp.) and coral bells. "Ruby-throats really respond to coral bells," he says, "even though they have such tiny flowers." He notes that another excellent nectar source is jewelweed. "It's not regularly grown in yards," he says, "but those who live on a lake often have it by accident. I always tell people that jewelweed is a good one to preserve."

Those gardeners fortunate enough to live in Minnesota's "Lake Country" attract large numbers of ruby-throats with relatively little effort. Mary and Les Brunker are one such couple. They live in a heavily forested area in Pequot Lakes, Minnesota. From spring through fall, they welcome so many ruby-throats to their lakeside yard that they can hear the hum of tiny wings while sitting outside. "It's just amazing," says Mary, "to see that many hummingbirds. They're out there all the time, wherever you look. And they're so bold! Sometimes when Les and I sit on the deck, a ruby-throat will zoom right between us.

"They'll even come up to me when I bring out a new jar of nectar. They'll start to drink from it as I'm walking across the deck." Because few flowers are in bloom when the ruby-throats return, the Brunkers greet the birds with two feeders, one in front and one in back of their house. They hang these in mid-May, about two weeks before the birds usually appear. They also set out potted plants and hanging flower baskets. "The ruby-throats especially like the impatiens and fuchsia," says Mary. "In fact, they *love* fuchsia. They also go to our browallia (*Browallia speciosa*), which has purple flowers."

The Brunkers maintain their feeders throughout the summer and into the fall and plant flowers for the birds in their patio area. "Every year, we plant annuals there such as petunia, begonia, impatiens and fuchsia," says Mary, "and the ruby-throats are on them right away. They'll check out all the plants, but the impatiens and the fuchsia are what they're really after."

The Brunkers also have a large wildflower garden with such ruby-throat favorites as cardinal flower, and the tiny birds have been seen to buzz about their vegetable garden as well.

Because of their wooded, lakeside location, the Brunkers attract a number of different birds, including orioles and woodpeckers, that sometimes raid the hummingbird feeders. "There's definitely a pecking order," says Mary. "The ruby-throats will sit in a tree and wait for the orioles to leave. And the woodpeckers boss them all! When the woodpeckers visit the feeders, they really suck the juice out. Meanwhile, the hummingbirds hover nearby, waiting their chance."

The Brunkers, who enjoy all wildlife, make no attempt to drive the larger birds away. Instead, they refill their feeders more frequently.

Several demonstration gardens at the Northland Arboretum in nearby Brainerd, Minnesota, give residents ideas on what they can plant at home. The arboretum features four hummingbird gardens, each about the size of an average yard. Biologist Pam Perry, who designed the gardens, notes that the birds seem especially fond of bee balm, coral honeysuckle, coral bells, blazing star (*Liatris* spp.), phlox and scarlet runner bean (*Phaseolus coccineus*). Last year, the

staff added a feeder as well, which instantly drew a number of hummers. Due to the feeder's success, they expect to hang more in the future.

A similar demonstration garden at the Ellis Bird Farm in Lacombe, Alberta, attracts ruby-throats as well. Biologist Myrna Pearman says that the tiny birds most often visit the bright blooms on the scarlet runner beans, which are trained to grow up a lattice. They also regularly drink from a variety of other plants, including scarlet sage, coral bells, columbine, bee balm, trumpet honeysuckle and nasturtium. She notes, however, that when they first arrive, they find very few flowers on which to feed, other than early-blooming lilacs and Siberian pea tree (*Caragana arborescens*).

Hummingbird enthusiast Tom Webb of Turner Valley, Alberta, echoes this observation. Every year, ruby-throats return to Webb's heavily wooded spread in mid-May. When they first arrive on his property, which is set on the Sheep River in the foothills of the Rockies, no flowers await them.

"There's really nothing blooming then," says Webb. "Even the berry bushes and the columbine and the bleeding heart don't bloom here until June. In fact, there's such an obvious lack of natural nectar that the ruby-throats have to be relying on insects instead."

Indeed, they feast on a treasure trove of protein-rich insects—in between visits to Webb's three feeders. "During the day," says Webb, "I'll see them work over the branches of the spruce trees, presumably gathering insects and maybe eggs and larvae. Then, in the evening, they'll sit on top of the spruce trees, just like flycatchers. They'll fly up and catch an insect and then come back down. I've even seen them hovering over the river, nailing the insects that go by."

Webb has attracted six species of hummingbirds to his 60 mostly wild acres, which straddle the ranges of eastern and western hummingbirds. Ruby-throats and rufous are the most common hummers in his yard, followed by the calliope. All three zip around his feeders every year. In addition, he welcomes occasional broad-tails, black-chins and, once, an Anna's. Sometimes the early arrivals must brave a snowstorm,

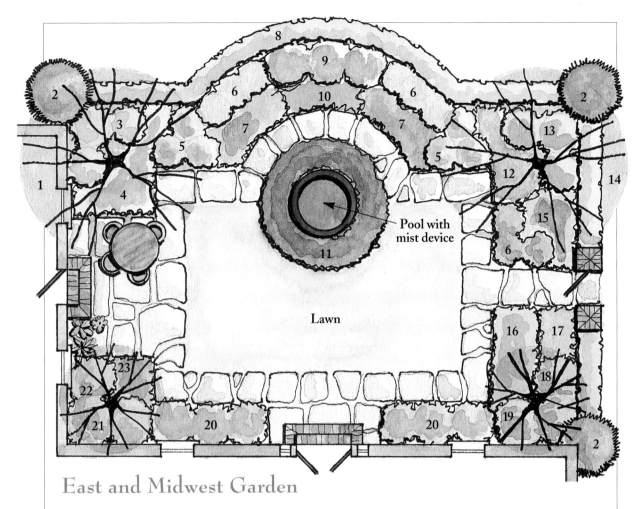

Pool with mist device

Lawn

East and Midwest Garden

1. Aesculus hippocastanum *horsechestnut*
2. *Evergreens*
3. Aesculus pavia *var.* pavia *red buckeye*
4. Monarda didyma *bee balm*
5. Symphoricarpos albus *snowberry*
6. Chaenomeles japonica *flowering quince*
7. Lobelia siphilitica *blue lobelia*

8. Syringa vulgaris *lilac*
9. Weigela florida *weigela*
10. Zinnia sp. *zinnia*
11. Salvia splendens *scarlet sage*
12. Kniphofia uvaria *red-hot-poker*
13. Elaeagnus umbellata *autumn olive*
14. Aesculus hippocastanum x carnea *red horsechestnut*
15. Mirabilis jalapa *four-o'clocks*

16. Phlox sp. *phlox*
17. Alcea rosea *hollyhock*
18. Rhododendron sp. *rhododendron*
19. Malus baccata *flowering crabapple*
20. Viburnum tinus *viburnum*
21. Phygelius capensis *Cape fuchsia*
22. Hibiscus syriacus *althaea*
23. Impatiens wallerana *impatiens*

although Webb notes that hummingbirds are so tough they don't seem to mind. "It's amazing to me how resilient hummingbirds are," he says, "especially when a snowstorm lasts two or three days."

Webb says that the hummingbirds that shoot about his yard "squabble and battle" all day. "But then, just before nightfall, they get along. At every feeder, you'll find a dozen or so waiting to drink."

Ruby-throats nest on Webb's property every year, usually choosing a site on a downturned spruce limb set under another, concealing, bough. Of the three nests he has found, two were built over water, which probably provides the birds with extra protection.

Every fall, the hardy little ruby-throats—males, females and their young—depart from Webb's property by mid-September. They will fly as far south as Costa Rica in search of tropical flowers and warm winter weather. Then in late February, they rev their tiny wings and begin their long, northward journey, enlivening gardens and wild places along the way.

CHAPTER ONE

Male Magnificent Hummingbird

A Master Guide to Hummingbirds

THE HUMMINGBIRD is among the most instantly recognizable of all feathered creatures. Because they require a high-energy diet of nectar, most people associate hummingbirds with vibrant gardens. Almost every region south of the Arctic—from desert to mountaintop—hosts one or more species, either as a resident or as a seasonal visitor. The 14 or so species that nest in the United States and Canada are a fragment of a very large tropical family, but they are the ones we know best—the ones that bring glamour and zest to our gardens.

In the following pages, we portray the lives of those species that regularly breed north of the Mexican border. Measurements given are averages of the total length, including the bill. Two species that nest only occasionally within that area and several others that occur infrequently are considered rarities and are not as likely to be found in many gardens. They are discussed in a more general manner after the species accounts.

ALLEN'S HUMMINGBIRD

Selasphorus sasin
Length: 3¾ inches

Description: The adult male Allen's hummingbird wears bronze-green feathers over his crown and back. Rufous color marks the nape and rump as well as the tail. A rufous wash covers the sides and undertail coverts. The gorget is vibrant orange-red, appearing golden, copper or green in some lights, and bordered below by pure white. In both the male and female plumages, the central tail feathers are the longest, giving the folded tail a pointed shape. The wings are dusky, while the bill is straight and black. The adult female is bronze-green above with a touch of rufous coloration in its tail. Its underparts are creamy white, washed with rufous on the flanks and undertail coverts. The outer three tail feathers on each side are tipped with white. A patch of iridescent orange-red feathers marks the center of the throat. The remainder of the throat is marked with rows of tiny dull green dots that give the appearance of an incoming gorget. The immature male closely resembles the adult female, but has a rufous rump and sometimes iridescent orange-red feathers on the sides of its incomplete gorget. The immature female is like the adult female, but has few, if any, dull green dots.

Identification: The adult male Allen's hummingbird is unmistakable with its bronze-green back, though a few individual rufous hummingbirds maintain a green cap and back and appear identical to Allen's males. The immature male and the female of any age cannot be reliably differentiated from rufous hummingbirds without capturing them to measure the widths of certain tail feathers.

Voice: Both the male and the female Allen's hummingbirds give a rather mechanical-sounding "*chp, chp, chp*" as a warning while feeding and when any other bird enters their territory. The note is given more rapidly as an intruder approaches more closely. In intense situations, numerous notes are strung together as a chatter. Vocalizations of this species are indistinguishable from those of the rufous hummingbird.

Courtship and Nesting: For the Allen's hummingbird, breeding takes place during the late winter and early spring months. The male flies a towering J-shaped display to attract the attention of any fe-

Male Allen's Hummingbird

male feeding within his territory and to assert his dominance to interloping males, of his own species or another.

The female chooses a site away from male territories to construct her nest. Oak trees seem to be favored, though cypress is also used. Sometimes the nest is built on a vine or the root of an overturned tree, and usually it is partially shaded from above. Manmade structures are occasionally chosen.

The female begins the nest by making a pad of

down secured with spider silk. Sometimes an old nest provides the support. Various materials may go into the main body of the nest—down from willows and asterlike flowers, hair from horses, dogs or even humans. The dull green exterior is covered with mosses or sometimes bits of grass or bark and, usually, lichens.

The first of the two dull white eggs is laid 8 to 11 days after nest-building commences, though the nest may not yet be completed. The second egg usually comes two days later. Incubation begins sometime after the laying of the first egg and lasts 17 to 22 days. Nesting materials are still added after incubation has begun and even until the young leave the nest.

The newly hatched young are tended by the female alone. Feathers begin appearing on about the seventh day. By the nineteenth day, the well-feathered nestlings are exercising their wings to practice for flight at about 22 to 25 days of age.

Behavior: The Allen's hummingbird is aggressive and quarrelsome, defending its feeding territory from all other hummingbirds. Insects, hawked from the air early in the morning or late in the evening, form a portion of the diet.

Habitat: The Allen's hummingbird is found in chaparral, thickets, brushy hillsides, canyons and ravines, and also in open coniferous woodland. In migration and in winter, members of this species may also forage in open landscapes with flowering shrubs. A large variety of flowers are visited by members of this species, including Indian paintbrush, California fuchsia and honeysuckle.

Range: Two populations of this species breed along the Pacific Coast, mostly in California. One resides year-round in the Channel Islands and on the Palos Verdes Peninsula of Los Angeles County. The other group is migratory and breeds from Santa Barbara County northward to southwestern Oregon.

The migratory population spends its nonbreeding months in Mexico. A few individuals have found their way to the Gulf Coast region, Tennessee and Massachusetts.

ANNA'S HUMMINGBIRD
Calypte anna
Length: 4 inches

Description: The Anna's hummingbird is notable for its glittering blue-green upper parts, husky build and straight black bill. Adult males sport iridescent rose-red crowns and rose-red gorgets. The underparts are dull gray with a wash of green on the sides and flanks that produces a scaly, vested appearance. The medium-length tail is primarily black and is slightly notched. The wings are dusky. Adult females usually have a spot of iridescent rose-red feathers in the center of the throat, a characteristic they share with immature males of their species. Otherwise, they are plain gray below. The base of their slightly notched tail is gray-green with a black band. The three outermost feathers on each side are broadly tipped with white. Immature males resemble the adult females but frequently have at least a few iridescent feathers on the crown. Immature females lack the central spot on the throat, at least when they are very young.

Identification: The Anna's hummingbird is larger than most other hummers within its range. The iridescent rose-red gorget and crown separate the male of this species from every other North American hummingbird. The female is similar in color pattern to the females (and immature males) of several other species, but it can be distinguished by its husky build, dingy gray breast and spot of iridescent rose-red feathers on the center of the throat. Rufous coloration is not present in any plumage of this species.

Voice: The male Anna's hummingbird sings a rather unmusical metallic warble as part of his courtship and as a territorial challenge. Members of both sexes issue a sharp, explosive *"tzip"* while feeding. Often the same note is given, but more rapidly, to express excitement or to warn territorial trespassers.

Courtship and Nesting: The courtship behavior of the Anna's hummingbird is the most extensively studied courtship behavior of any hummingbird species in North America. The male stakes out a territory centered on a stand of flowers rich with nectar, where he sings and performs a towering display flight that includes an explosive squeak at the lowest point. This display also serves to intimidate rivals. The female enters the territory to feed and is chased by the male.

After the brief but intense chase, the male performs a smaller, more fervent display, called a "shut-

Male Anna's Hummingbird

tle," in front of the perched female. While perching, he delivers a passionate little song, then mounts the female and mates with her.

Immediately after mating, the female preens and rearranges her feathers before returning to her nest-building. Dense oak groves in wooded canyons are favored locations, but a wide variety of sites have been recorded, including many on and around human dwellings. The typical nest, constructed in about seven days, is made of plant downs held together with spider webs. Small feathers sometimes line the inside, while a camouflage of lichens is added after the female begins her 14- to 19-day incubation.

The female broods and tends the young in the nest for a period of 18 to 23 days. She continues to feed the fledglings for a week or so, but they are soon independent enough to find their own food. Often the female mates again and begins a second brood soon after the young of a first nest are on their own.

Behavior: Members of this species are not truly migratory, at least not in the manner of other hummingbirds. Courtship and nesting begin during the winter months of November and December, a period when members of most migratory species are on their tropical wintering grounds. After nesting is completed in the late spring, many Anna's hummingbirds wander into areas where they do not breed.

Habitat: Anna's hummingbirds seem more adaptable to manmade environments than most other species, frequently nesting around human habitations. But they are also found in open woodland, chaparral, scrubby areas and partly open situations. After breeding, some Anna's hummingbirds ascend to mountainous regions in response to the peak flowering of favored plants. Red-flowering currant and fuchsias provide much of the nectar during the breeding season, while tree tobacco is much sought in the summer.

Range: The Anna's hummingbird is best known as a species of the Pacific slope of North America. It is the most widespread and abundant member of its family on the West Coast, where it breeds from western Washington south to northwestern Baja California in Mexico. Anna's hummingbirds also breed in southern Arizona. It is thought that Anna's hummingbirds have expanded their range since the 1950s, perhaps as a result of increased suburbanization and its complementary exotic plantings. In recent years, there have been numerous sightings far north and east of the regular range in Arkansas, Louisiana, Alabama, Florida and Minnesota.

BLACK-CHINNED HUMMINGBIRD

Archilochus alexandri

Length: 3¾ inches

Description: The black-chinned hummingbird is recognized by its glittering dark green upperparts and its purple-bordered black gorget. This species exhibits a very long black bill and a deeply notched black tail. The underparts are dull gray-white, shading to pure white just below the gorget. A dull green wash covers the flanks. The wings are blackish. The adult female lacks a gorget and has white tips to the three outermost feathers of her tail, which is rounded on each side. The underparts are dull gray-white. The immature male resembles the adult female, though he may show dusky stipples on his throat and may have a few iridescent purple feathers. Buffy edges to the feathers of the upperparts mark immatures of both sexes. Otherwise, the immature female is identical to the adult female.

Identification: The male black-chinned hummingbird can be mistaken for the male of several other species if all of the field marks are not seen well. It shares a purple gorget with both the Costa's and the Lucifer hummingbirds, but unlike the Costa's, the black-chinned hummingbird has a dusty green rather than purple crown. The gorget of the black-chinned hummingbird is neat and rounded, while the gorget of the Lucifer hummingbird has long feathers projecting out from the sides. The immature male appears longer billed and longer tailed than the immature male Costa's, and it lacks the touch of rufous in the tail of the immature male Lucifer. The ruby-throated hummingbird is about the same size and shape as the black-chinned hummingbird, and if seen in poor

light, the gorget of the ruby-throated hummingbird can appear black.

The female black-chinned hummingbird is very similar to the female of several other species, especially the Costa's hummingbird and the ruby-throated hummingbird. The bill of the female black-chinned hummingbird is longer and heavier than the bills of the other two species and is sometimes slightly decurved. Generally, the underparts of the female black-chinned are a shade darker and dingier than those of the other two species. The black-chinned hummingbird is found in similar habitats to the Costa's hum-

Male Black-chinned Hummingbird at Ocotillo, Fouquieria splendens

mingbird, and its range overlaps that of the ruby-throated hummingbird in central Texas.

Voice: Adult male black-chinned hummingbirds sometimes sing a faint warble while perched. While feeding and when in the presence of other hummingbirds, members of both sexes give a soft, plaintive "*tchew*," similar to the note given by the ruby-throated hummingbird.

Courtship and Nesting: The male black-chinned hummingbird flies a stylized, wide U-shaped display in his territory to impress females and intimidate rivals. The female, if she is receptive, perches low in a shrub while the male moves closer and begins a smaller version of the display, called a "shuttle."

The female black-chinned hummingbird uses spider webbing to secure her nest of plant down to a slender, downward-slanting twig (sometimes in a fork) in a tree. Many types of trees seem to be acceptable, but oaks seem to be preferred. Lichens, as well as bud scales, stamens, bits of bark and flowers may camouflage the outer surface of the nest. The nest may be located near human activities. Nancy Newfield found one under construction a few feet above the driveway of a busy church parking lot in Austin, Texas.

The female incubates her two white eggs for 13 to 16 days. After the eggs hatch, the naked young are brooded and fed by the female. At the age of about three weeks, the now well-feathered young leave the nest and are soon independent. The female continues to feed the fledglings for a few days until they learn to forage for themselves. She may mate again and begin another nest while still tending dependent young.

Behavior: Small flying insects compose a portion of the diet of the black-chinned hummingbird. Often, one may see an individual sally forth from a perch and trace intricate designs through a cloud of nearly invisible gnats. Frequently, while hovering, the black-chin pumps and fans its tail furiously, a behavior that is quite distinctive.

Habitat: The black-chinned hummingbird uses a variety of habitats over its extensive range from open woodlands to desert washes to chaparral, parks and gardens. Favorite flowers include ocotillo, desert honeysuckle and tree tobacco in the arid regions this species prefers.

Range: The black-chinned hummingbird is widespread as a breeding species in the western United States from eastern Washington, central Idaho and northwestern Montana south through eastern Wyoming, eastern Colorado, New Mexico, central and southern Texas and west to California. A portion of the range is in northern Mexico.

After the nesting season, most members of this species migrate south into Mexico, though some individuals spend the winter months along the Gulf Coast and in Florida. Occasionally a few birds stray far north and east of the usual range for the species.

BLUE-THROATED HUMMINGBIRD
Lampornis clemenciae
Length: 5 inches

Description: The blue-throated hummingbird is one of the largest hummingbirds in North America. The adult male blue-throated hummingbird is bronze-green on its crown, nape and back, shading into bronze on the rump. A white line or streak extends backward from the eye. The white streak is bordered below by a dusky patch, producing a masked effect. The gorget is deep iridescent blue, varying in hue according to the angle of light. The gorget is sometimes bordered by an indistinct white stripe. The remainder of the underparts are clear gray. The large tail is black, glossed with metallic blue, and the outer three tail feathers are broadly tipped with white. The wings are dusky. The long, straight bill is black. The females, both adult and immature, resemble the adult male but are gray on the throat instead of blue. The immature male shows some blue feathers on its throat from an early age.

Identification: Size alone is sufficient to separate members of this species from all others except the magnificent hummingbird, with which it shares a considerable part of its range. Colors of the adult males of the two species are distinctively different. The blue gorget, white postocular line and conspicuous white patches on the corner of the large, frequently fanned black tail separate the male of this species from the overall dark magnificent hummingbird. The blue-throated hummingbird is the only North American species in which the adult male shows white in its tail.

The female blue-throated hummingbird and the female magnificent hummingbird are somewhat similar to each other in appearance. The female blue-throated hummingbird is distinguished by its darker gray underparts, dusky mask, white line behind the eye and large white patches on the corners of the tail.

Voice: The blue-throated hummingbird is very

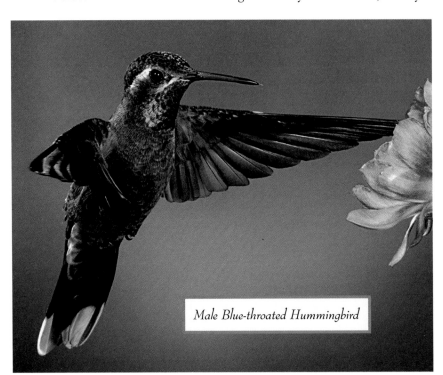

Male Blue-throated Hummingbird

vocal, uttering a high-pitched "*seek*" in flight and while feeding. According to Dr. Alexander Wetmore in a 1932 *National Geographic Magazine*, "males sing a simple song of three or four notes, repeated at short intervals while the singer perches upright with head elevated."

Courtship and Nesting: The male element of courtship has, apparently, not been well described. In the mountains of southeastern Arizona, the blue-throated hummingbird nests from late April through the middle of July. The female constructs a bulky (for a hummingbird) nest of a variety of natural materials, including oak catkins and stems, green mosses, coarse straws, weed stems and plant downs. The sturdy nest is woven together with cobwebs and decorated on the outside with mosses and lichens. Plant down lines the interior. It is sometimes fastened to the stems of shrubs growing from canyon walls in the rugged terrain that members of this species inhabit.

Nests holding the one or two unglossed white eggs have frequently been found in and about human dwellings and outbuildings.

Behavior: The blue-throated hummingbird is a bold bird, usually dominating other hummingbirds at food sources. Even the equally large magnificent hummingbird defers to its aggressive style. In Portal, Arizona, blue-throated hummingbirds perch in oaks overlooking the feeders at the home of Drs. Walter and Sally Spofford. From this vantage point, they wait to ambush other birds, especially the smaller black-chinned hummingbirds.

These birds call frequently while feeding and when in conflicts with other hummers. Insects, gleaned from vegetation and hawked from the air, form a large part of the diet.

Habitat: Within its range in the United States, the blue-throated hummingbird inhabits open woodlands, especially pine-oak and deciduous, and second growth in moist canyons at rather high elevations. In migration, blue-throated hummingbirds visit gardens in more open locales. Favorite flowers include *Penstemon*, cardinal flower and tree tobacco.

Range: The range of the blue-throated hummingbird lies mainly in Mexico. In the United States, breeding is limited to a few mountain ranges in southeastern Arizona and southwestern New Mexico and the Chisos Mountains of western Texas. A female, far out of range in south-central California, mated with either an Anna's hummingbird or a black-chinned hummingbird and raised young in 1977 and 1978. After the nesting season, vagrants have been found in Utah, Colorado, northern New Mexico, along the Texas coast and in Louisiana.

BROAD-BILLED HUMMINGBIRD

Cynanthus latirostris

Length: 4 inches

Description: The beautiful male broad-billed hummingbird is vibrant from the tip of its bright coral-red bill to the end of its glossy blue-black tail. Its crown and back are bronze-green. A pale spot or streak extends behind the eye. A glittering sapphire blue throat shades into green on the breast and belly. Tufts of pure white surround the legs, and the feathers under the tail are also frequently pure white. The long, ample black tail is rather deeply notched. The wings are blackish. The adult female is more subdued in color, being bright grass-green on its crown and back and medium gray below. There are scattered green spots on the sides. Dark feathers behind and below the eye, bordered above and below by lighter gray feathers, give the appearance of a mask. The female's bill is mostly black, with a varied amount of pink or orange at the base. Her tail is mostly dark with dull gray tips to the outer feathers. The wings are brownish. The immature male resembles the female, but shows some blue and green on the underparts.

Identification: The male broad-bill is fairly easily identified, because its colors are so distinctive, but an observer noticing only the pale streak behind the eye may confuse members of this species with the smaller, and much more rare, white-eared hummingbird. Similarly, the female shows a pale streak behind the eye, which may give the impression of a white line, and may therefore cause misidentification.

Voice: The call most frequently associated with the broad-billed hummingbird is a loud, raspy "*je-dit,*" given by both males and females under a variety of circumstances. In courtship, the male emits a metallic "*chnk.*" A young male in winter was recorded singing a barely audible, high-pitched warble.

Courtship and Nesting: The male broad-billed hummingbird uses a simple display to attract the attention of the female. According to William Baltosser, who spent several seasons studying the birds in Guadalupe Canyon, in Arizona and New Mexico, the male swings back and forth in a very shallow pendulum close to his prospective mate, all the while "revving" his wings and producing a distinctive sound.

Nesting covers a long season, and two broods may be produced. A female in Guadalupe Canyon began a second nest while still tending large nestlings. The nest is composed of a variety of materials, including plant down and grass stalks. Outer decorations may

Male Broad-billed Hummingbird

be of bits of bark and leaves, and sometimes blossoms. Spider webbing binds the structure to a fine, drooping twig or vine, frequently near the ground and close to a stream bed. The broad-billed hummingbird breeds prodigiously in the well-studied Madera Canyon, Arizona, where two nests photographed were situated in poison ivy.

According to Baltosser, incubation requires about two weeks. The nestlings are tended for 21 to 22 days before they fledge, after which they are fed for an additional week, perhaps slightly longer.

Behavior: The broad-billed hummingbird is bold and curious, frequently approaching the observer and hovering with much movement of its large tail. In search of a meal, these hummers probe many kinds of flowers and take a wide selection of gnats, plant lice, leafhoppers, parasitic wasps, spiders and pollen grains. Interactions with other species of hummingbirds are frequent while the birds are foraging.

Habitat: The broad-billed hummingbird is found in arid scrub, semidesert and open deciduous woodland. Within its limited range in the United States, it seeks nectar from ocotillo, century plant and tree tobacco.

Range: Most of the range of the broad-billed hummingbird lies in Mexico, but members of this species are common in the deserts and wooded canyons of southeastern Arizona and southwestern New Mexico. Occasionally, they are seen in California and Texas, and there are a few exceptional records from Louisiana.

BROAD-TAILED HUMMINGBIRD

Selasphorus platycercus
Length: 4 inches

Description: The elegant broad-tailed hummingbird is strikingly blue-green on its cap, back and central tail feathers. The adult male wears a gorget of rose-magenta and has an indistinct wash of green on its flanks. A shrill trill caused by attenuated outer wing feathers is characteristic. The adult female lacks the gorget, but may have a few rose-magenta feathers on her throat. A wash of pale cinnamon covers her flanks. As the species' name implies, the tail is long and ample, with white tips marking the outer three feathers of the female. The immatures of either sex resemble the adult female. Neither the female nor the immature male produce the typical wing sound of the adult male.

Identification: The adult male broad-tailed hummingbird is distinguishable from other male hummingbirds by the combination of its rounded gorget, green crown, pale underparts and long, squared tail with a touch of rufous coloration. The male Anna's hummingbird has a rose-colored crown as well as a rose-colored gorget with extensions on the sides, gray underparts with a dark green wash and a short, slightly notched tail with no rufous coloration. The male calliope hummingbird is much smaller and has very long extensions to the sides of its more magenta gorget. To many people, the male broad-tailed resembles the male of the ruby-throated hummingbird, but the reds of the gorget and greens of the back of the two species are very different shades. The ruby-throated hummingbird's short black tail, which shows no rufous coloration, is deeply notched instead of squared.

The female broad-tailed hummingbird is similar to the female of several other species, especially the calliope, rufous and Allen's hummingbirds. But, the female broad-tailed hummingbird is larger, with a noticeably longer and wider tail. The amount of rufous coloration in the tail is less than that of either the rufous or Allen's hummingbird and the central tail feathers are green to the end, not edged with dull black.

Voice: The male broad-tailed hummingbird does not sing but rather issues a musical "*chirp*" to warn of territorial intrusion. The female gives a similar call when contesting nesting and feeding areas. It gives a faint "*chirp*" when leaving its nest and when feeding solitarily.

Courtship and Nesting: The courting male broad-tailed hummingbird gives a spectacular dive display, followed by a closer, more intimate display, the shuttle, in the presence of a female. Hovering at the top of the dive may help the male to spy potential rivals as well as to impress the nearby female.

After mating, the female constructs her nest in four or five days, using plant materials and saddling it on a limb with spider webbing or silk from cocoons.

Male Broad-tailed Hummingbird

The cup may vary considerably in size from one nest to another. Usually, the interior is cushioned with down from willow or cottonwood, while the exterior may be covered with lichens, bark or fine grasses. Sometimes materials are pilfered from the nests of other hummingbirds; frequently, repairs and additions are accomplished during incubation. A successful nest site may be used in succeeding years by the same female.

Hatching occurs after a 16- to 19-day incubation period that begins before the second egg is laid. The female warms the chicks with her body until they are 10 to 12 days old. She feeds them a diet rich in gnats and aphids. The entire nesting process requires about six weeks.

Behavior: The broad-tailed hummingbird spends much of its time perched on a high snag that permits aerial surveillance of the territory. A series of high climbs and dives that resemble the breeding display is effective to intimidate intruders, which they do not hesitate to chase from their territories. Flycatchers,

grosbeaks and hawks are assaulted with as much enthusiasm as are other hummers.

These hummers are known for their curiosity and boldness, often investigating items about campsites. Dr. E.A. Mearns, quoted in *Life Histories of North American Cuckoos, Goatsuckers, Hummingbirds and their Allies* by Arthur Cleveland Bent, described the travails of a member of his camping party who wore a scarlet cap. Constant attacks became so troublesome that the cap was eventually pocketed in order to be rid of the "irate little furies."

Habitat: The broad-tailed hummingbird inhabits open woodlands with oaks, pines and junipers in mountainous areas during its nesting season. In migration and winter, it may also be found in open situations with flowering shrubs. Members of this species seek nectar from a variety of plants such as scarlet mint, bouvardia and columbine.

Range: The mountains of the western states from central Idaho, northern Utah and northern Wyoming south through western Texas, Colorado, New Mexico, Arizona and southeastern California are home to nesting populations of broad-tailed hummingbirds. These birds migrate south into Mexico after nesting. A few may be found in the Gulf Coast region from Texas to Alabama in winter, and one has been reported in Georgia.

BUFF-BELLIED HUMMINGBIRD

Amazilia yucatanensis
Length: 4¼ inches

Description: The buff-bellied hummingbird is distinguished by its bronze-green upperparts, glittering emerald-green throat and chest, and cinnamon-buff belly. The long ample tail is a rich chestnut color and is slightly notched. The wings are dusky. The long, heavy and slightly decurved bill is coral-colored with a dusky tip. A narrow buff-colored eye ring gives members of this species a big-eyed appearance. Unlike most other members of its family in North America, males and females are similar in appearance, though females are less brightly colored than adult males. Young birds resemble their parents, but feathers on the throat and breast have buffy edges, producing a scaled appearance. The tips of their bills show more dark color than those of adults.

Identification: The colors of this species are strikingly different from those of any other regularly occurring North American hummingbird. Superficially, the buff-bellied resembles the very rare berylline hummingbird that visits and occasionally nests in the mountains of Arizona. But that species is slightly smaller and has a less brightly colored bill than the buff-bellied humming-

bird, and it shows considerable rufous coloration in the wings. The rufous-tailed hummingbird, a widespread tropical species, also sports similar colors and has been said to have occurred in southern Texas, although scientifically acceptable proof of its occurrence has not been put forth. That species is slightly larger than the buff-bellied and has a squared, not notched tail. Its underparts are gray rather than buff, and its song and call are markedly different.

Voice: A chatter sounding like electric static is given when the bird is disturbed and in aggressive encounters. Gerry Green of Nursery, Texas, has watched buff-bellieds for many years. She describes the song, given from a perch, as five or six clear notes that descend in pitch. This song is seldom heard and its role in the courtship is not understood, as the species has apparently not been thoroughly studied. Other elements of the courtship are not well known.

Male Buff-bellied Hummingbird

Courtship and Nesting: Gerry Green has witnessed a flight that she believes relates to breeding. From high up in the air, the male flew higher, then came down at bullet-like speed into a deep, wide arc. The female builds her nest three to eight feet from the ground in small trees or bushes. Anacahuita is a favorite, while hackberry and willow are also used. According to Major C.E. Bendire, quoted in *Life Histories of North American Cuckoos, Goatsuckers, Hummingbirds and their Allies* by Arthur Cleveland Bent, the two pure white eggs are laid in a nest made of shreds of vegetable fiber, thistledown and a vegetable substance much like cattle hair. The outside is covered with bits of dried flower petals, shreds of bark and pieces of light-colored lichens, securely fastened by spider webs. The nest is usually saddled on a small, drooping limb or placed in a fork of a horizontal twig. Outside dimensions are 1¼ inches high by 1⅜ inches wide on average. Details of incubation period and behavior, brooding behavior and fledging period have not been published.

Behavior: The buff-bellied is noisy yet somewhat reclusive and is often heard before coming into view. It prefers to perch deep within a shrub, usually at no great height, and darts out to defend its territory rather than striking from an exposed perch. Flight is swift, though wingbeats are slower than those of most smaller species, giving it an odd jerky movement.

Habitat: In southern Texas, the buff-bellied hummingbird is found in dense thickets overgrown with flowering shrubs and vines, a habitat that has diminished greatly with the development of large-scale agriculture in that region. It is thought that habitat destruction is responsible for a decline of this species. They also frequent gardens lush with tropical foliage. Favorite flowers include anacahuita, turk's cap and mesquite.

Range: The buff-bellied hummingbird is primarily a Mexican species, reaching the northernmost limit of its breeding range in the Lower Rio Grande Valley of Texas. Reports of individuals in late spring and early summer from as far north as Corpus Christi and Victoria suggest local nesting. The species has been little studied in the United States.

In fall and winter, many members of this species move away from their breeding habitats. The majority migrate south into Mexico, but a number of them fly northward and spend the winter months along the Gulf Coast in eastern Texas and southern Louisiana. The species has been reported from most states bordering the Gulf of Mexico and there are exceptional records from far inland in central Texas and Arkansas.

CALLIOPE HUMMINGBIRD
Stellula calliope
Length: 3¼ inches

Description: The calliope hummingbird is the smallest of all hummingbirds found in the United States and Canada. The magenta gorget feathers of the adult male are long and form stripes that stand out against a background of pure white. When not extended, the gorget feathers lie flat, obscuring the underlying white. The calliope hummingbird's upperparts are iridescent blue-green, sometimes shading to yellow-green. The underparts are dull white with a slightly greenish wash on the flanks of the adult male. The adult female lacks a gorget and shows pale cinnamon flanks. The wings are brownish. The short, straight, needlelike bill is black. The short, somewhat squared tail is blackish on the adult male. The tail of the female is blackish, with the outer three feathers on each side tipped with white. Inner tail feathers show cinnamon edges. The immatures resemble the adult female, though the immature male may sport a few colored gorget feathers.

Identification: The adult male calliope hummingbird is easily recognized when seen well, but the females and the immature male are more difficult to distinguish. The small size is obvious when direct comparison can be made with members of other species, but this is often not possible. Members of several species that occur within the same general range of the calliope may resemble it. The female broad-tailed hummingbird is much larger and has a large tail that appears tapered, not squared, when folded. The female rufous hummingbird has a bronze-green back and a tapered, not squared, tail. The female black-chinned hummingbird has a very long bill and shows no cinnamon on the tail feathers. In all plumages, the wings extend to the tail tip and often beyond. The combination of short bill and short tail gives members of this species a stubby look.

Voice: The calliope hummingbird is rather quiet but vocalizes while feeding and during aggressive interactions. The voice, audible at rather close range, is a soft "*tik.*" In courtship, the male gives a flat "*bzt*" at the lowest point of his U-shaped dive.

Courtship and Nesting: The male relies on a dazzling U-shaped display flight accompanied by an explosive metallic "*tzing*" to impress a prospective

Male Calliope Hummingbird

mate. The female selects a site on a small twig beneath a sheltering larger branch on which to construct her nest. Conifers are frequently chosen, and the materials blend well with the site. The outside is made of tiny leaves, mosses and bark and is held together with spider silk. The nest is lined with plant downs, frequently those of cottonwood or willow.

The two eggs may be laid before the nest is completed. Incubation lasts about 15 days, after which the

female tends the young for about three weeks before they are mature enough to leave the nest.

Behavior: The calliope hummingbird is most usually found at very high elevations, often to the timberline, where it has been observed feeding at penstemons and paintbrushes. It is a pugnacious bird and defends its territory vigorously against larger hummers. Insects, hawked from the air, make up a part of their diet. Some observers have noted a tendency for members of this species to perch and feed close to the ground.

Habitat: The tiny calliope hummingbird is an inhabitant of mountain meadows, forests and willow and alder thickets through most of its breeding range, though in the more northern and eastern regions it occupies much lower altitudes. In winter and in migration, the calliope hummingbird is also found in lowland scrub, deserts and other arid regions. Paintbrush, lousewort and snowplant are frequent nectar resources.

Range: The calliope hummingbird is found nesting from central British Columbia and southwestern Alberta south through Washington, Oregon, Nevada and California to the northern part of Baja California in Mexico and east to northern Wyoming and Utah.

Migration away from breeding areas takes most of the population south into southern Mexico. In recent years, individuals have been recorded wintering in the Gulf Coast region from Louisiana to Florida. There are exceptional records of stray calliope hummingbirds from Nebraska, Kansas, western and central Texas and Minnesota.

COSTA'S HUMMINGBIRD

Calypte costae

Length: 3½ inches

Description: The male Costa's hummingbird is recognized by its sparkling purple gorget and crown. The back is a dull green. The dark brown tail is slightly indented in the center. The underparts are pale gray-white with a light green wash on the flanks. The female Costa's hummingbird lacks the purple gorget and crown and the green wash on its flanks. Its underparts are pale gray-white and its tail has white tips to the three outermost feathers on each side. Sometimes a few purple feathers mark the throat. The immature male resembles the female but often shows purple feathers near the corners of its future gorget.

Identification: The adult male Costa's hummingbird is easily distinguished from the male of the other purple-gorgeted species—the black-chinned and Lucifer hummingbirds—if its iridescent purple crown can be seen. The female and immature Costa's hummingbird may be confused with the female or the immature male of several other species. Generally, the female and immature male Costa's hummingbirds are paler overall, with shorter bills and tails than the black-chinned hummingbirds of the same sex and age. They are generally paler and much smaller than the Anna's hummingbirds of the same sex and age. A dusky patch below and behind the eye is surrounded by pale feathers, producing a vaguely masked appearance. Both Costa's and black-chinned hummingbirds, but not the Anna's hummingbird, tend to pump their tails rapidly up and down while hovering to feed. The female and immature Costa's hummingbirds also resemble the ruby-throated hummingbirds of the same sex and age, but members of the two species almost never occur in the same geographical region and habitat.

Voice: The chip note of the Costa's hummingbird is a high-pitched "*tik*," often given many at a time, sounding like a twitter when the bird is excited. The song is described by well-known researcher F. Gary Stiles as "a high, thin whistle."

Courtship and Nesting: The Costa's hummingbird times its breeding season to take advantage of the desert flowers that appear after late winter rains in February or March. The male Costa's hummingbird uses a series of impressive dive displays accompanied

Male Costa's Hummingbird

by a shrill, prolonged vocalization to excite the female. Sometimes, a smaller, more intimate shuttle is also performed. Mating takes place while the female is perched.

The female Costa's hummingbird builds her nest in a wide variety of locations from numerous species of trees to shrubs, yuccas, cacti and weeds. Materials are considerably more varied than those used by females of other species and include down from various plants, scales of buds or flowers, thin strips of bark, bits of gray lichens and string. As usual for hummingbirds, spider webs are used to bind the structure together and to anchor it in place. The interior is lined with soft plant down and sometimes small, soft feathers. The outside is covered or partially covered with small feathers or leaves. The nest may be near water, but often it is not.

Incubation lasts for 15 to 18 days, beginning with the first egg. The young remain in the nest for 20 to 23 days before they are ready to fly. After fledging, young Costa's hummingbirds are fed by the female for a week or more, according to Peter Scott, who has studied the birds in the deserts of Arizona and California. He noted that only on rare occasions will a female raise a second brood.

Behavior: Members of this species are less dependent on the presence of water than are most other hummingbirds. The male Costa's hummingbird likes to survey his arid domain from a high, exposed perch where he often sings and calls. From this vantage point, he can chase away any intruders. His territorial ire may be directed against members of his own species, other hummingbirds or even species that offer no competition for food or mates.

Habitat: The Costa's hummingbird nests in deserts and semideserts, arid foothills and chaparral. Outside of the breeding season, members of this species are also found in adjacent mountains, open meadows and gardens. Ocotillo is an important nectar source, as is desert willow and tree tobacco.

Range: A part of the Costa's hummingbird range is in Mexico, but in the United States they breed from central California, southern Nevada and southwestern Utah south to southern Arizona and southwestern New Mexico. After nesting, they occur in southern California and southern Arizona. Occasional individuals have wandered as far north as southern Alaska and as far east as the Texas coast.

LUCIFER HUMMINGBIRD
Calothorax lucifer
Length: 3½ inches

Description: The Lucifer hummingbird is most notable for its very long, slightly decurved black bill. The adult male wears a shimmering, regal purple gorget that is greatly elongated on the sides. Its deeply forked black tail is usually kept folded, giving the tail a spiky appearance. Bronze-green feathers cover the crown, back and rump of the adults of both sexes and

Male Lucifer Hummingbird

of immature birds. The wings are dusky. The female of any age and the immature male have buffy underparts that may vary in hue from bright to pale. The female Lucifer hummingbird has a dusky patch below and behind the eye, giving it a masked appearance. The immature male resembles the female but shows a few colored gorget feathers by late summer.

Identification: The Lucifer hummingbird is not likely to be confused with any other hummingbird if it is studied well, but members of two other desert-dwelling species exhibit similarities that could confuse the unfamiliar. The males of two other species, the black-chinned hummingbird and the Costa's hummingbird, also have purple gorgets. But the male black-chinned hummingbird does not have elongated sides to its gorget, and the male Costa's hummingbird has an iridescent purple crown as well as a purple gorget. Neither of the two males has a long, spiky-looking tail.

The female Lucifer hummingbird has a very long, decurved bill and buffy underparts. The bills of the females of several other species may also show a slight curvature, and their gray-white underparts may be discolored with pollen. The female Lucifer differs from the female black-chinned by having a longer tail with a little rufous coloration. Similar differences exist between the female Lucifer and the female Costa's hummingbirds, and the female Costa's hummingbird has a shorter bill. Both the male and the female Lucifer hummingbirds perch with a characteristic hunched posture.

Voice: The Lucifer hummingbird gives a dry "*tic*" note that is sometimes repeated several times. A more musical "*tsi-chip*" is given by the female while in a male's territory or when a male approaches her nest, and also by a male when approaching a female on her nest. Both adult and immature males give a thin, wheezy call "*brrzhee! brrzhee,*" audible only at close range on returning to their perches.

Courtship and Nesting: In courtship, the male Lucifer hummingbird is unique in that it seeks out the female on the nest and there performs a display consisting of a side-to-side flight, called a "shuttle," followed by a vertical climb culminating in a single powerful dive, after which it flies rapidly away in a zigzag manner with the tail spread. During the shuttle flight, the gorget feathers are extended and a sound reminiscent of a deck of cards being shuffled is produced. A description of actual mating has not been published.

In Texas, where Peter Scott has intensively studied the birds, the female constructs a cup-shaped nest from oak catkins, flowers of snakecotton and acacia, composite pappus and leaves, bound together with spider webs—all gathered within a few hundred feet of the site—on a cholla cactus or a dead lechugilla stalk. Sometimes, a new nest is constructed on top of a nest remaining from the previous year. The female frequently steals nesting material from other active nests.

She incubates her two white eggs for about 15 days, then feeds the nestlings a diet rich in small spiders for 19 to 24 days. The female continues to feed the newly fledged young for another 13 to 19 days. It is not unusual for a female Lucifer hummingbird with dependent young to begin construction of a new nest in a different location and mate again if nectar supplies are abundant.

Behavior: The male Lucifer hummingbird uses a display that resembles an incomplete breeding flight to defend its territory, which may be centered on nectar plants. It chases males, females and immatures of its own species as well as any other hummingbirds from the area. The female guards the vicinity of her nest from other female hummingbirds and from possible predators, such as orioles and shrikes. After nesting, males, females and young may defend territories centered on abundant desert honeysuckle. At other times, however, the Lucifer hummingbird may be nonterritorial.

Habitat: In the Big Bend region of western Texas, the Lucifer hummingbird breeds on arid plateaus and rugged mountain slopes that have scattered ocotillo, sotol and century plants—remote desert haunts that will likely remain free of degradation from humans. Outside of the breeding season, members of this species are found in a wide elevational range. Century plant, penstemon and desert honeysuckle provide much of the nectar they consume.

Range: Most Lucifer hummingbirds live in Mexico, although small migratory populations nest in Big Bend National Park (Texas) and in the Peloncillo Mountains (New Mexico). At times, others are found elsewhere in western Texas, southwestern New Mexico and southeastern Arizona. Occasional strays have been seen north and east of these regions within the same states.

MAGNIFICENT HUMMINGBIRD

Eugenes fulgens
Length: 5¼ inches

Description: The magnificent hummingbird is notable for its large size and dark beauty. The adult male sports an iridescent blue-violet crown and glittering emerald-green gorget. The back and slightly notched tail are brass-green. The breast and belly are blackish, shading to grayish on the flanks. The very long, sturdy bill is black. The wings are blackish. The female, which lacks the glittering crown and gorget colors, can be recognized by her large size. Her underparts are uniformly pale gray. The tips of the outer three tail feathers are grayish.

The immature male resembles the adult female but shows some of the male colors. The immature female is nearly identical to the adult female but has buffy or grayish edges to the feathers of her upperparts.

Identification: If it is seen well, there is no difficulty in distinguishing the adult male magnificent hummingbird from any other hummingbird in the United States. No other hummer has an iridescent green throat as well as a glittering purple crown, and only the much different blue-throated hummingbird is nearly as large.

The female magnificent hummingbird is somewhat similar in appearance to the female blue-throated hummingbird. It can be distinguished from the blue-throat by its paler gray underparts and its lack of a distinct white line behind the eye. The gray tips to the outer three tail feathers are considerably smaller and less noticeable than the large white tips on the outer three tail feathers of the blue-throat's tail.

Voice: The vocalization of the magnificent hummingbird can best be described as a loud, rather musical "*chrp.*"

Courtship and Nesting: The male courtship ritual seems not to have been described. The female magnificent hummingbird selects the nesting site on a horizontal twig fairly high in any of numerous species of trees. The nest resembles a larger version of that of the ruby-throated hummingbird and is fashioned in about a week's time from soft, silky plant fibers and mosses, bound together with spider silk. It is lined with soft plant down and sometimes fluffy feathers.

Male Magnificent Hummingbird

The outside is covered with lichens. Two eggs are laid, but beyond that, nothing seems to have been published concerning incubation or maternal care.

Behavior: As befits its large size, the magnificent hummingbird is aggressive and confrontational. Nancy Newfield and Mahlon Ayme watched as an irascible male defended a roadside stand of thistle in the Huachuca Mountains of Arizona. A small flock of lesser goldfinches was attempting to feed on the seeds that had already developed, but the magnificent hummingbird attacked from above and rode the back of each tiny yellow bird until he had cleared the area of interlopers.

Instead of maintaining a flower-based territory through the breeding season, as many other species do, magnificent hummingbirds defend their feeding area for a little while, then move on to another successively, a strategy called traplining. Members of this species also consume many insects and spiders, which they catch around sycamores and pines.

Habitat: The magnificent hummingbird is most often found in and at the edges of humid forests and open woodlands. Members of this species sometimes forage in scrubby areas and clearings. Flowering century plants and penstemons provide nectar.

Range: Most of the range of the magnificent hummingbird is south of the United States in Mexico and Central America, but they are found breeding in southeastern Arizona, southwestern New Mexico and western Texas and have occasionally bred in western Colorado. After nesting, most of the birds disperse and migrate south into Mexico, though a few pass the winter months in Arizona. Occasional strays have been reported from as far north as southwestern Canada, Michigan and Minnesota and as far east as Arkansas, Alabama and Georgia.

RUBY-THROATED HUMMINGBIRD

Archilochus colubris
Length: 3¾ inches

Description: The ruby-throated hummingbird is known for its brilliant red gorget and glittering emerald-green crown and back. Shading on the gorget may vary from ruby-red to gold or green, depending on the angle of reflected light, and the upperparts may appear yellow-green. In poor light, the gorget may appear black. The underparts are dull white, washed on the sides with drab green. The deeply notched tail is black, as is the long, slender bill. The wings are dusky. The female lacks the red gorget and the green wash on its sides. Its tail is somewhat larger and is rounded on each side, with the three outer tail feathers marked with white tips. The immature is like the adult female, though the young male may show a few iridescent red feathers on its throat.

Identification: The adult male ruby-throated hummingbird wears a similar color pattern to the adult male broad-tailed hummingbird, but the latter is larger and has a squared, not notched, tail marked with a touch of rufous color. Its green upperparts are blue-green rather than emerald, and its gorget is rose-red rather than ruby. The male Anna's hummingbird is larger and has extensions to the sides of its gorget as well as having an iridescent red crown. The male black-chinned hummingbird is similar to the ruby-throated hummingbird in size and shape, but it has a black and purple gorget that appears black in poor light. To identify a hummingbird properly, care must be taken to see the color of the gorget.

The female ruby-throated hummingbird is similar to the female of several other species, most notably the black-chinned and Costa's hummingbirds. The female black-chinned hummingbird has a longer, heavier bill and more dingy gray underparts. The female Costa's hummingbird has a dusky area on its face that extends behind and below the eye. That area is bordered by pale feathers, giving the face a masked appearance. The Costa's hummingbird almost never occurs in the same geographical region and habitat as the ruby-throated hummingbird.

Voice: The ruby-throated hummingbird gives a petulant "*tchew*" note when in the presence of other hummers and especially when feeding. During intense interactions with other hummingbirds, the notes are frequently run together. Sometimes, a squeal is emitted during an aggressive chase, though it is not known if the bird squealing is the pursuer or the pursued.

Courtship and Nesting: The male ruby-throated hummingbird uses a dramatic flight to trace an invisible U in the air, followed by a closer, more intimate side-to-side flight, the shuttle, to allure his prospective mate during courtship. He produces a mechanical buzz when closest to the female.

The female gathers soft plant down and bud scales

Male Ruby-throated Hummingbird at Belize Sage, Salvia miniata

to construct the compact nest, which she lashes to a slender twig with spider silk. Lichens, some of which are added after incubation has begun, cover the outside, providing excellent camouflage. Usually, she chooses a site that slants downward, frequently over or near water. Overhanging branches shelter the structure and its precious contents from sun and rain. Fabrication may take as little as a single day, but it more often requires about a week.

The two white eggs are warmed by the female for about 16 days, beginning before the laying of the second egg. The young are fed tiny insects and nectar for about three weeks before they are able to leave the nest.

Behavior: The ruby-throated hummingbird, a familiar visitor to eastern gardens, is inquisitive, investigating every flower, regardless of color, to find the best food sources. Though red flowers are selected more frequently than those of other colors, any blossom that is found to satisfy will draw a clientele.

Members of both sexes are aggressive in the defense of their territories, whether they are centered on flowers or the nest.

Habitat: The ruby-throated hummingbird nests in a variety of habitats, including deciduous and mixed woodlands, swamps, parks and open situations with scattered trees. It frequently seeks nectar in nearby gardens and meadows. When migrating and during the winter, they find food in many habitats, especially open scrubby areas with a few trees. Japanese honeysuckle, trumpet creeper and jewelweed draw many individuals.

Range: The ruby-throated hummingbird nests over a vast region, including most of the eastern United States and Canada north to southern Manitoba, southern Ontario, southern Quebec, New Brunswick, Prince Edward Island and Nova Scotia. More northerly breeding birds range westward to central Alberta and central Saskatchewan. The western edge cuts through the eastern portions of the

Dakotas, Nebraska and Kansas and the central portions of Oklahoma and Texas.

Most ruby-throated hummingbirds spend their nonbreeding months in Mexico and Central America south to central Costa Rica, mostly on the Pacific slope. Southern Florida and the Gulf Coast region from Texas to western Florida host a small number through the winter. Isolated individuals have been found in early winter within the breeding range. Stray birds have wandered as far west as Alaska, California, New Mexico and western Texas.

RUFOUS HUMMINGBIRD

Selasphorus rufus

Length: 3¾ inches

Description: The rufous hummingbird is recognized by its rich rusty hue and fiery temperament. The adult male wears noniridescent rufous feathers over its crown, back and tail. A wash of the same color covers the sides and undertail coverts. The gorget is vibrant orange-red, appearing golden, copper or green in some lights, and bordered below by pure white.

The adult female is bronze-green above with a touch of rufous coloration on its tail. Its underparts are creamy white washed with rufous on the flanks and undertail coverts. The outer three tail feathers on each side are tipped with white.

In both the male and female plumages, the central tail feathers are the longest, giving the folded tail a tapered shape. A patch of iridescent orange-red feathers marks the center of the female's throat. The remainder of the female's throat is marked with rows of tiny dull green dots that give the appearance of an incoming gorget. The wings are dusky, while the bill is straight and black.

The immature male closely resembles the adult female but can be distinguished by having a rufous rump and sometimes iridescent orange-red feathers on the sides of its incomplete gorget. The immature female is like the adult female, but has few, if any, dull green dots.

Identification: The adult male rufous hummingbird is unmistakable with its rusty back; however, a few individuals maintain a green cap and back, and these birds appear identical to males of the closely related Allen's hummingbird. The immature male that has not attained its rufous back and the female of any age cannot reliably be differentiated from the Allen's hummingbird without capturing it to measure the widths of certain tail feathers.

Voice: Both the male and the female rufous hummingbirds give a rather mechanical-sounding "*chp, chp, chp*" as a warning while they are feeding or when another bird enters their territory. The note is given more rapidly as an intruder approaches more closely. In intense situations, numerous notes are strung together as a chatter.

Male Rufous Hummingbird at Paintbrush, Castilleja *sp.*

Courtship and Nesting: The male rufous hummingbird performs a stylized display flight to attract the attentions of the female, which perches low in vegetation within the male's feeding territory. Actual mating has not been described. The male displays for several females in succession.

The female rufous hummingbird constructs its nest of soft, downy plant materials fastened together with spider webbing and decorated on the outside with lichens, bark fragments and mosses. The nest is usually well hidden in a variety of shrubs and trees, sometimes on a sheltered bank, and usually protected by overhanging boughs. Occasionally, several females build in close proximity to each other, an unusual circumstance for such territorial birds.

Incubation requires 15 to 17 days, with one young hatching a day before the other. The female alone feeds a high-protein diet of insects to the nestlings, which gape and call in response to air moving from the beating of the female's wings. The young begin to practice flying when they are about 15 days old and preen themselves a few days later. The entire nesting cycle lasts about six weeks.

Behavior: The rufous hummingbird is noisy and intensely territorial, defending its feeding area with great vigor. The males use a display similar to courtship flight to intimidate rivals for possession of a prime location. The female and young fan their tails while hovering and facing intruders, seemingly to highlight the rufous color of their tails. Members of this species prefer to guard their territories from a high exposed perch.

Habitat: Coniferous forests, brushy hillsides, thickets and older second growth are suitable for the breeding rufous hummingbird. Feeding may be in adjacent scrubby areas and meadows. When migrating and during the winter, members of this species use many open areas where flowers are present. Favorite flowers include flowering currant, red columbine and salmonberry.

Range: The rufous hummingbird is the most northerly breeding hummer, nesting from southern Alaska south through southern Yukon, western British Columbia, southwestern Alberta, western Montana, eastern Oregon and central Idaho to northwestern California.

Most rufous hummingbirds migrate south to central Mexico for the winter months, but many spend their nonbreeding season along the Gulf Coast from Texas to Florida. Additionally, isolated individuals winter in coastal southern California. Rufous hummingbirds disperse widely after nesting. There are numerous reports of members of this species from the eastern United States and Canada and an exceptional record from extreme eastern Russia.

VIOLET-CROWNED HUMMINGBIRD
Amazilia violiceps
Length: 4½ inches

Description: The exquisite male violet-crowned hummingbird has a dusky tip to its vivid coral-red bill. The crown is glittering royal purple and the back is dull bronze. The underparts—throat, breast, belly—are pure white. The tail is olive-green and the wings are brownish. The adult female is similar to the adult male, but it is slightly duller in color. Immatures of both sexes are similar as well but show buffy edges to feathers on the crown and rump, giving them a distinctly dull appearance.

Identification: No other hummingbird in the United States shows such a striking combination of colors—a glittering purple crown with a dull, bronze back, gleaming white underparts and a bright red bill. However, overeager birders in the canyons of Arizona sometimes mistake female black-chinned or broad-billed hummingbirds, with their grayish underparts, for members of this species. Both of those species are also considerably smaller than the violet-crowned.

Voice: The vocalization of the violet-crowned hummingbird is described by William Baltosser, who has studied them nesting in Guadalupe Canyon, in New Mexico and Arizona, as a chatter not unlike that of the broad-billed hummingbird. According to Baltosser, one can produce a similar sound by gently shaking two steel ball bearings in a closed hand.

Male Violet-crowned Hummingbird

broad-billed, black-chinned, rufous and Costa's hummingbirds. In that habitat, their larger size gave the violet-crowned hummingbirds a clear advantage.

Habitat: The violet-crowned hummingbird prefers open woodland and scrubby edges of forest, riverside groves and plantations. Members of this species have been observed sampling nectar from numerous kinds of flowers, including tree tobacco and century plant.

Range: In the United States, the violet-crowned hummingbird is limited as a breeding species to Guadalupe Canyon, which originates in the extreme southwestern corner of New Mexico and crosses the extreme southeastern corner of Arizona. Elsewhere in Arizona, they are regularly found along Sonoita Creek and at the Paton's feeders in Patagonia, and often in Ramsey and Madera Canyons. There are isolated sightings in other parts of Arizona and from California and Texas.

Courtship and Nesting: The manner in which the male violet-crowned hummingbird courts has not been well described. Baltosser noted a male chasing a female and heard "considerable chattering." For her part, the female builds her nest in five to ten days using bristles from asterlike flowers and long, plumose styles from *Clematis ligusticifolia* (western virgin's bower) and *Fallugia paradoxa* (Apache plume). Spider webs bind the creation to a slender twig. A few pale green lichens serve to camouflage the outside. All nests recorded in the United States have been fairly high in Arizona sycamore trees. Incubation lasts about 14 days. The female tends the dependent young for 21 to 22 days before they leave the nest and for another week or two afterward.

Behavior: In Baltosser's study, violet-crowned hummingbirds fed heavily from the flowers of century plants, which they dominated in competition with

RARITIES

The hummingbirds most likely to visit your garden are the ones that occur most commonly in your region. Occasionally, a visitor from another area may wander into your domain, making it a rarity for your state or province, though not rare within its accustomed range.

Once a bird strays from its usual haunts, it may wander a considerable distance in search of familiar terrain and flowers. More and more frequently, unusual hummingbirds are appearing in areas where they had never before been seen, exciting news for the hummingbird gardener.

The **rufous hummingbird** regularly deviates from its normal migration route in the Rocky Mountains and has been recorded in many eastern states. Hummingbirders in the Gulf Coast region now expect to see them in fall and winter. Members of other species are being reported with increasing frequency as well.

Most of the hummingbird species in neighboring Mexico and the islands of the Caribbean region are not migratory in the same sense as those that breed in more northerly latitudes, but many disperse from breeding areas in response to changing patterns of available nectar in favored blossoms. Young birds, finding all the suitable habitats occupied by adults of their species, may search for other areas in which to take up residence. Some species may be extending their ranges, while others may be reacting to a loss of

Berylline Hummingbird

habitat. Whatever the reason, hummingbirders in the border states and in Florida may find a visitor from outside the United States and Canada. Birders in Ari-

zona and Texas search for glittering strays from Mexico every year.

The striking **white-eared hummingbird** (3¾ inches long) is reported almost every year from southeastern Arizona, where it probably nests, at least occasionally, in some remote canyons. It is also seen from time to time in New Mexico and western Texas. The adult male has a royal purple crown and chin, an emerald-green throat and a wide stripe of snow-white behind the eye, bordered below by a black ear patch. The bill is coral-red. The adult female is more subdued in color, lacking the glittering purple, but she also has a wide white stripe behind the eye, bordered below by a black ear patch. Her throat and sides are spotted with green and blue-green. Her bill is mostly black, though a bit of coral-red shows at the base.

The **berylline hummingbird** (4¼ inches long) is reported almost every year in the mountains of southeastern Arizona near the Mexican border, where it has nested several times. It has also been seen in New Mexico and, possibly, Texas. The adult male is glittering green above and below. The lower belly, rump, tail and wings are chestnut, and the base of the bill shows a little red. The adult female is similar to her mate but lacks some of his brilliance, and she has a gray rather than chestnut lower belly.

Another semiregular visitor to Arizona is the **plain-capped starthroat** (5 inches long), an inhabitant of scrubby arid foothills in its native Mexico. The adult male has a small red gorget that is bordered by a white whisker stripe, white tufts on its flanks and a very long black bill. The adult female resembles the adult male, but has a smaller gorget.

The elegant **green violet-ear** (4¾ inches long) strays to Texas from time to time but has also found its way to such far-flung locales as Alabama, Arkansas, North Carolina and Ontario. The adult male is mostly shimmering green, with large patches of blue-violet on the chest and sides of the face. When agitated, the green violet-ear fans the patches on its face outward. The female has a similar appearance.

In the late nineteenth century, a period of natural history exploration in the American West, the **bumblebee hummingbird** (3 inches long) was recorded in Arizona and the **rufous-tailed hummingbird** (4 inches long) was recorded in Texas. Neither has been reliably sighted since the initial reports. At this time, it cannot be known if these species were accurately identified in the first place or if no additional members of these two species found their way to the United States.

The Texas occurrence of an **Antillean crested hummingbird** (3½ inches long), a resident of Puerto Rico, the Virgin Islands and the Lesser Antilles, cannot be explained by any pattern of natural vagrancy. Equally puzzling was the presence of a female **Xantus' hummingbird** (3½ inches long) from southern Baja California, in Mexico, that attempted to nest in Ventura County, California. No one knows why a female in breeding condition would stray so far from others of her kind.

The **Bahama woodstar** (3½ inches long), a resident throughout the Bahama Islands, has been found several times in southern Florida. The **Cuban emerald** (4 inches long), a resident of Cuba and the Bahamas, has been reported in Florida on several occasions. It is not certain that the identifications are beyond question, however, because several other Caribbean species are similar in appearance.

In 1992, an immature **green-breasted mango** (4½ inches long) appeared in Texas. This large, husky hummer had an iridescent purple tail and a dark iridescent stripe down its otherwise white breast and belly. A stunning hummer, the green-breasted mango is native to Mexico and Central America. Other members of this species have been reported feeding from the small-flowered sultan's turban that grows wild along much of the Texas coast.

A **cinnamon hummingbird** (4 inches long) was

Male White-eared Hummingbird

photographed in Arizona in 1992. This species, which is related to the buff-bellied hummingbird, is usually found in arid scrub on the Pacific slope of Mexico and Central America. Another member of the same species appeared in New Mexico the following year.

The appearance of a rarity is exciting and unexpected. Any hummingbird gardener who finds a hummer that is out of the ordinary should contact other birders, their local chapter of the National Audubon Society and members of the nearest ornithological society. Information about such birds may aid in our understanding of these fascinating creatures.

CHAPTER TWO

Powder Puff, Calliandra sp.

A Master Guide to Hummingbird Plants

CA = California, excluding the eastern mountain region

PW = Pacific Northwest, Pacific Canada, Alaska

SW = Southwest

WM = Western Mountains, including Canadian Rockies

SE = Southeast, including eastern and southern Texas

EM = East and Midwest, including eastern Canada

TREES

	CA	PW	SW	WM	SE	EM
Aesculus hippocastanum horsechestnut	CA	PW		WM	SE	EM
Aesculus hippocastanum x *carnea* red horsechestnut		PW		WM	SE	EM
Albizia julibrissin mimosa, silk tree	CA	PW			SE	EM
Arbutus menziesii madrone	CA	PW				
Arbutus unedo strawberry tree	CA	PW			SE	
Arbutus xalapensis var. *texana* Texas madrone					SE	EM
Bauhinia variegata orchid tree	CA				SE	
Brachychiton bidwillii Australian bottle tree	CA					

Callistemon viminalis weeping bottlebrush	CA		SW	SE	
Caragana arborescens Siberian pea tree					EM
Carnegiea gigantea saguaro			SW		
Chilopsis linearis desert willow	CA		SW		
Citrus spp. citrus	CA		SW	SE	
Cordia sebestena geiger tree				SE	
Delonix regia royal poinciana	CA		SW	SE	
Embothrium coccineum Chilean flame tree		PW			
Eriobotrya japonica Japanese plum, loquat	CA			SE	
Erythrina 'Bidwillii', *Erythrina* spp. coral tree	CA		SW	SE	
Erythrina crista-galli cry-baby tree	CA			SE	
Eucalyptus cladocalyx sugar gum	CA			SE	
Eucalyptus ficifolia red-flowering gum	CA			SE	
Eucalyptus globulus blue gum	CA			SE	
Eucalyptus lehmannii Lehmann's gum	CA			SE	
Eucalyptus leucoxylon white ironbark	CA		SW	SE	
Eucalyptus maculata spotted gum	CA			SE	
Eucalyptus mannifera var. *maculosa* red-spotted gum	CA			SE	
Eucalyptus melliodora yellow box	CA			SE	
Eucalyptus polyanthemos silver-dollar gum, silver-dollar tree	CA			SE	
Eucalyptus robusta swamp mahogany	CA			SE	
Eucalyptus sideroxylon red ironbark	CA		SW	SE	
Grevillea robusta silk oak	CA		SW		
Liriodendron tulipifera tulip tree	CA	PW	WM	SE	EM
Malus baccata, *M. floribunda* flowering crabapple	CA	PW	WM	SE	EM
Prunus autumnalis flowering cherry		PW			EM
Robinia pseudoacacia black locust	CA	PW	WM	SE	EM
Sophora tomentosa necklace pod, silverbush				SE	EM
Telopea oreades Australian flame tree		PW			
Ungnadia speciosa Mexican buckeye, Texas buckeye			SW		

SHRUBS

Abelia floribunda Mexican abelia	CA			SE	
Abelia grandiflora glossy abelia					EM
Abutilon hybridum, *A. pictum* flowering maple	CA			SE	
Abutilon megapotamicum trailing flowering maple	CA			SE	
Aesculus pavia var. *pavia* red buckeye		PW	WM	SE	EM
Agapetes serpens	CA				
Agave chrysantha, *A. deserti*, *A. parryi*, *A. americana*, *A. scabra* century plant, giant century plant	CA		SW	SE	

Red-flowering Gum, Eucalyptus ficifolia

Texas Olive, Cordia boissieri

Camellia, Camellia sasanqua

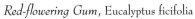

Anisacanthus thurberi, *A. quadrifidus* var. *wrightii* desert honey-suckle, Mexican honeysuckle, hummingbird bush, chuparosa	CA		SW	SE	
Arctostaphylos spp. manzanita	CA	PW	SW	WM	
Bouvardia ternifolia scarlet bouvardia	CA		SW	SE	
Buddleia alternifolia butterfly bush, summer lilac	CA	PW		WM	SE	EM
Buddleia davidii summer lilac, orange-eye			SW	
Caesalpinia gilliesii bird of paradise	CA		SW	SE	
Caesalpinia pulcherrima Barbados' pride, Mexican palo verde, dwarf poinciana, Mexican bird of paradise	CA		SW	SE	
Calliandra californica Baja fairy duster	CA		SW	
Calliandra eriophylla fairy duster	CA		SW	
Calliandra spp. powderpuff	CA			SE	
Calliandra tweedii Trinidad flame bush, Mexican flame bush	CA		SW	SE	
Callistemon citrinus, *C. speciosus* bottlebrush	CA	PW	SW	SE	
Calothamnus spp. net bush	CA			
Camellia sasanqua camellia, sasanqua	CA	PW		SE	
Ceanothus arboreus mountain lilac	CA			
Ceanothus fendleri California lilac, buckbrush	CA			
Cephalanthus occidentalis buttonbush		PW		WM	SE	EM
Ceratostigma willmottianum Chinese plumbago	CA			
Cestrum elegans cestrum	CA			SE	
Cestrum parqui willow-leafed jessamine	CA			SE	
Chaenomeles speciosa, *C. japonica* flowering quince	CA	PW	SW	WM	SE	EM
Clerodendrum speciosissimum pagoda plant, glory-bower	CA			SE	
Cochemiea setispina cactus			SW	
Cordia boissieri anacahuita, Texas olive			SW	SE	
Correa pulchella, *C. neglecta*, *C. reflexa* Australian fuchsia, correa	CA			
Cuphea ignea, *C. micropetala*, *C.* 'David' Mexican cigar	CA		SW	WM	SE	
Duranta repens pigeon berry, skyflower, golden dewdrop	CA		SW	SE	
Echinocereus triglochidiatus, *E. engelmannii* hedgehog cactus	CA		SW	

Echium 'Pride of Madeira'	CA				
Elaeagnus umbellata autumn olive		PW		WM	EM
Erica mammosa 'Jubilee', *E.* spp. South African heath, heather	CA	PW			
Erythrina flabelliformis western coral bean			SW		
Erythrina herbacea coral bean	CA			SE	
Escallonia exoniensis 'Frades'	CA				
Fouquieria splendens ocotillo	CA		SW		
Fuchsia lycioides, *F. magellanica*, *F.* 'Marinka', *F.* 'Gartenmeister Bonstedt', other species and hybrids (singles)	CA	PW		WM	EM
Galvezia speciosa bush snapdragon	CA				
Grevillea spp., *G.* 'Robyn Gordon'	CA			SE	
Hakea spp.	CA		SW		
Hamamelis virginiana common witch hazel	CA	PW			EM
Hamelia patens firebush			SW	SE	
Hedychium coccineum x *coronarium* peach ginger	CA			SE	
Hedysarum coronarium French honeysuckle		PW			
Heliconia bihai macaw flower				SE	
Hesperaloe nocturna white hesperaloe			SW		
Hesperaloe parviflora red yucca	CA		SW		
Hibiscus coccineus red star hibiscus, Texas star				SE	
Hibiscus rosa-sinensis hibiscus, Chinese hibiscus, rose of China	CA			SE	
Hibiscus syriacus althaea, rose of Sharon	CA	PW		WM SE	EM
Iochroma cyaneum	CA				
Isomeris arborea bladderpod	CA		SW		
Jasminum nudiflorum winter jasmine		PW			
Justicia brandegeana shrimp plant	CA	PW	SW	SE	
Justicia californica chuparosa	CA		SW		
Justicia carnea Brazilian plume	CA			SE	
Justicia ovata red justicia, everblooming justicia			SW	SE	
Justicia spicigera orange jacobinia, orange justicia, Mexican honeysuckle, hummingbird bush	CA		SW	SE	
Kolkwitzia amabilis beauty bush	CA	PW		WM	EM
Lambertia formosa honey flower	CA				
Lantana camara, *L. horrida*, *L. montevidensis* lantana	CA		SW	WM SE	
Lavatera assurgentiflora tree mallow	CA	PW			
Leucophyllum frutescens ceniza, barometer bush, Texas ranger	CA		SW		
Lonicera involucrata twinberry honeysuckle	CA	PW		WM	
Lonicera tatarica tatarian honeysuckle				WM	EM
Lycium spp. wolfberry			SW		
Mahonia aquifolium Oregon grape	CA	PW		WM	

Plant	CA	PW	SW	WM	SE	EM
Malvaviscus arboreus var. *drummondii* sultan's turban, turk's cap, turk's head	CA		SW		SE	
Malvaviscus arboreus var. *mexicanus* giant turk's cap, turk's cap	CA				SE	
Melaleuca spp.	CA		SW			
Melianthus major honey bush	CA					
Nicotiana glauca tree tobacco	CA		SW		SE	
Odontonema strictum firespike	CA				SE	
Opuntia imbricata chain-link cactus			SW			
Pachystachys coccinea cardinal's guard	CA				SE	
Pachystachys lutea golden shrimp plant, golden candle	CA				SE	
Pedilanthus macrocarpus candelilla			SW		SE	
Penstemon cordifolius red bush penstemon, honeysuckle penstemon	CA					
Polygala dalmaisiana sweet pea shrub	CA				SE	
Protea mellifera sugar bush, honey flower	CA					
Rhipsalidopsis gaertneri Easter cactus	CA		SW		SE	
Rhododendron canescens wild azalea		PW			SE	EM
Rhododendron serrulatum swamp azalea					SE	
Rhododendron spp. rhododendron, azalea		PW			SE	EM
Ribes aureum golden currant	CA	PW		WM		EM
Ribes cereum wax currant				WM		
Ribes indecorum white-flowered currant		PW				
Ribes laxiflorum trailing black currant		PW				
Ribes lobbii	CA	PW				
Ribes malvaceum chaparral	CA					
Ribes sanguineum crimson-flowered currant, gooseberry	CA	PW				EM
Ribes speciosum red-flowering currant, fuchsia-flowered currant	CA	PW				
Robinia hispida moss locust, rose acacia					SE	EM
Rubus procerus Himalaya berry		PW				
Rubus spectabilis salmonberry		PW				
Russelia equisetiformis fountain plant, firecracker plant	CA				SE	
Salvia leucantha Mexican bush sage	CA		SW		SE	
Salvia regla mountain sage	CA		SW		SE	
Schlumbergera bridgesii Christmas cactus	CA		SW		SE	
Schlumbergera truncata Thanksgiving cactus	CA		SW		SE	
Strelitzia reginae bird of paradise	CA				SE	
Symphoricarpos albus snowberry	CA	PW		WM		EM
Syringa vulgaris lilac		PW		WM		EM
Tecoma stans yellow bells, trumpet bush	CA		SW		SE	
Tecomaria capensis Cape honeysuckle	CA		SW		SE	

Templetonia retusa coralbush	CA				SE	
Torricula peria sticky nama	CA					
Trichostema lanatum woolly blue-curls	CA					
Vestia lycioides vestia		PW				
Viburnum tinus, *V.* 'Bodnantense' laurustinus, viburnum		PW			SE	EM
Weigela florida cardinal shrub	CA	PW			SE	EM

Hegdehog Cactus, Echinocereus *sp.*

Bladderpod, Isomeris arborea

Chinese Hibiscus, Hibiscus rosa-sinensis

PERENNIALS AND ANNUALS

Agapanthus orientalis lily of the nile	CA				SE	
Agastache berberi giant hummingbird mint	CA	PW	SW	WM	SE	EM
Agastache cana double-bubble mint	CA	PW	SW	WM	SE	EM
Agastache mexicana hyssop, giant hyssop	CA	PW	SW	WM	SE	EM
Alcea rosea hollyhock	CA	PW		WM	SE	EM
Aloe barbadensis aloe vera	CA		SW		SE	
Alstroemeria psittacina Peruvian lily	CA				SE	EM
Anigozanthos sp. kangaroo paw	CA				SE	
Antirrhinum majus snapdragon	CA	PW		WM	SE	EM
Aquilegia caerulea blue columbine	CA	PW		WM	SE	EM
Aquilegia canadensis, *A. elegantula* wild columbine	CA	PW		WM	SE	EM
Aquilegia chrysantha golden columbine			SW			
Aquilegia formosa western columbine	CA	PW		WM	SE	EM
Asclepias curassavica Mexican milkweed	CA		SW		SE	
Asclepias tuberosa butterfly milkweed, butterfly weed	CA		SW	WM	SE	EM
Beschorneria yuccoides	CA		SW			
Calamintha coccinea red basil					SE	
Canna spp. and hybrids canna lily	CA	PW	SW	WM	SE	EM
Castilleja coccinea, *C. integra*, *C. miniata*, *C.* spp. Indian paintbrush, painted cup	CA	PW	SW	WM		EM
Chelone glabra, *C. lyonii* turtlehead, pink turtlehead						EM
Cirsium arizonicum Arizona thistle, other spp.			SW			

Mexican sunflower, Tithonia rotundifolia — Wild bergamot, Monarda fistulosa — Crocosmia, Crocosmia 'Lucifer'

Name	CA	PW	SW	WM	SE	EM
Cirsium vulgare bull thistle		PW				
Crocosmia 'Lucifer' montbretia, crocosmia	CA			WM	SE	EM
Cynoglossum grande western hound's tongue	CA	PW				
Delphinium cardinale scarlet larkspur	CA	PW		WM		
Delphinium nudicaule, D. nelsonii and other spp. larkspur	CA	PW		WM	SE	EM
Dicentra spectabilis, D. eximia bleeding heart		PW		WM		EM
Dierama gracile, D. pendulum, D. pulcherrimum wandflower	CA	PW				
Digitalis spp. foxglove	CA	PW		WM	SE	EM
Epilobium angustifolium fireweed		PW		WM		EM
Epimedium grandiflorum bishop's hat	CA	PW	SW	WM		
Gladiolus spp. gladiolus, sword lily	CA			WM	SE	EM
Hemerocallis hybrids daylily	CA	PW	SW	WM	SE	EM
Heuchera sanguinea coral bells	CA	PW	SW	WM	SE	EM
Hosta spp. hosta, plantain lily		PW		WM	SE	EM
Impatiens capensis jewelweed, *I. pallida*, spotted jewelweed					SE	EM
Impatiens wallerana impatiens, patient Lucy, busy Lizzie	CA	PW	SW	WM	SE	EM
Ipomopsis aggregata scarlet gilia, skyrocket	CA	PW		WM		
Ipomopsis rubra standing cypress			SW	WM	SE	EM
Iris spp. iris	CA	PW		WM	SE	EM
Kalanchoe 'Flaming Katy' kalanchoe	CA		SW		SE	
Kniphofia uvaria red-hot-poker, tritoma	CA	PW		WM	SE	EM
Leonotis leonurus lion's ear	CA		SW		SE	
Liatris spp. gay feather, blazing star	CA			WM		EM
Lobelia cardinalis, L. laxiflora cardinal flower	CA	PW	SW	WM	SE	EM
Lobelia siphilitica blue lobelia, blue cardinal flower				WM		EM
Lycopus americanus bugleweed		PW				
Mertensia virginica Virginia bluebells, cowslip	CA				SE	EM
Mimulus cardinalis, M. longiflorus, M. puniceus, M. brevipes, M. spp. monkey flower	CA		SW	WM		
Mirabilis jalapa four-o'clock	CA	PW	SW	WM	SE	EM

Species	CA	PW	SW	WM	SE	EM
Mirabilis multiflora desert four-o'clock				WM		
Monarda didyma, M. citriodora bee balm, bergamot	CA	PW	SW	WM	SE	EM
Monarda fistulosa horsemint, wild bergamot			SW	WM	SE	EM
Monardella macrantha	CA					
Penstemon barbatus scarlet bugler	CA	PW	SW	WM		EM
Penstemon bridgesii	CA	PW		WM		EM
Penstemon cardinalis cardinal penstemon	CA	PW	SW	WM		EM
Penstemon centranthifolius scarlet bugler	CA	PW	SW	WM		EM
Penstemon eatonii Eaton's penstemon, firecracker penstemon	CA	PW	SW	WM		EM
Penstemon harvardii Harvard penstemon			SW			
Penstemon newberryi mountain pride	CA	PW		WM		EM
Penstemon ovatus	CA	PW		WM		EM
Penstemon palmeri	CA	PW	SW	WM		EM
Penstemon parryi Parry's penstemon	CA	PW	SW	WM		EM
Penstemon pinifolius pineleaf penstemon	CA	PW		WM		EM
Penstemon procerus	CA	PW		WM		EM
Penstemon pseudospectabilis	CA	PW	SW	WM		EM
Penstemon spectabilis	CA	PW	SW	WM		EM
Penstemon strictus Rocky Mountain penstemon, porch penstemon	CA	PW		WM		EM
Penstemon subulatus	CA	PW	SW	WM		EM
Penstemon superbus			SW			
Penstemon ternatus	CA	PW		WM		EM
Penstemon virens blue-mist penstemon	CA	PW		WM		EM
Penstemon wrightii Wright's penstemon	CA	PW		WM		EM
Pentas lanceolata pentas, Egyptian star	CA				SE	
Phlox spp. phlox	CA	PW		WM	SE	EM
Phormium tenax New Zealand flax	CA	PW				
Phygelius capensis Cape fuchsia	CA	PW		WM	SE	EM
Physostegia virginiana obedient plant	CA	PW		WM	SE	EM
Rubus spp. raspberry	CA	PW		WM		EM
Salvia clevelandii Cleveland sage	CA		SW			
Salvia coccinea Texas sage, tropical sage, scarlet sage	CA		SW	WM	SE	EM
Salvia elegans pineapple sage	CA	PW	SW	WM	SE	EM
Salvia greggii Rocky Mountain sage, autumn sage	CA		SW	WM	SE	
Salvia guaranitica anise sage, giant blue sage	CA	PW			SE	EM
Salvia henryi			SW			
Salvia lemmoni Lemmon's sage			SW			
Salvia mexicana	CA				SE	
Salvia miniata Belize sage	CA				SE	
Salvia spathacea pitcher sage	CA					

Salvia splendens red salvia, scarlet salvia, scarlet sage	CA	PW	SW	WM	SE	EM
Salvia vanhouttii	CA				SE	
Saponaria officinalis bouncing bet, soapwort						EM
Silene californica California Indian pink	CA					
Silene laciniata Indian pink, Mexican campion				WM		
Silene virginica fire pink					SE	EM
Spigelia marilandica Indian pink, pinkroot					SE	EM
Stachys coccinea scarlet hedge nettle, scarlet betony, Texas betony, red mint	CA		SW	WM		
Symphytum spp. comfrey	CA	PW		WM	SE	EM
Thermopsis divaricata golden banner				WM		
Tithonia diversifolia, T. rotundifolia Mexican sunflower	CA		SW	WM	SE	EM
Tropaeolum tuberosum, T. speciosum nasturtium	CA	PW		WM	SE	EM
Watsonia beatricis bugle lily	CA	PW			SE	
Zauschneria californica, Z. cana California fuchsia, hummingbird trumpet	CA	PW	SW	WM		
Zinnia spp. zinnia	CA	PW	SW	WM	SE	EM

VINES AND RAMBLERS

Asarina antirrhinifolia snapdragon vine	CA		SW			EM
Bignonia capreolata cross vine				WM	SE	EM
Campsis radicans trumpet creeper, trumpet vine	CA	PW	SW	WM	SE	EM
Clematis ligusticifolia western virgin's bower	CA	PW		WM		EM
Clerodendrum thompsoniae bleeding heart	CA				SE	
Columnea spp. and hybrids columnea	CA				SE	
Eccremocarpus scaber Chilean glory flower	CA	PW			SE	EM
Ipomoea coccinea red morning glory				WM	SE	EM
Ipomoea multifida cardinal climber	CA				SE	
Ipomoea quamoclit cypress vine	CA		SW		SE	
Lonicera arizonica Arizona honeysuckle			SW			
Lonicera ciliosa orange honeysuckle	CA	PW		WM		
Lonicera interrupta chaparral honeysuckle	CA					
Lonicera japonica Japanese honeysuckle, Hall's honeysuckle	CA	PW	SW	WM	SE	EM
Lonicera sempervirens coral honeysuckle, trumpet honeysuckle	CA		SW	WM	SE	EM
Mandevilla laxa Chilean jasmine	CA				SE	
Manettia cordifolia, M. inflata firecracker vine	CA	PW			SE	
Phaseolus coccineus scarlet runner bean	CA		SW	WM	SE	EM
Senecio confusus Mexican flame vine	CA		SW		SE	
Tropaeolum peregrinum canary bird vine	CA	PW		WM		

Information Sources for Plant List: American Birding Association Convention: "Hummingbird Workshop," by Nancy L. Newfield; "Attracting Hummingbirds to the Denver Landscape," from the Denver Audubon Society; "How To Create Your Own Backyard Wildlife Habitat," from the Washington Department of Wildlife; "Hummingbird Garden," from the Washington Department of Wildlife; "Hummingbirds and how to attract them," from the Washington Department of Wildlife; "Hummingbirds in Your Garden," from the Arizona-Sonora Desert Museum; "Hummingbirds: Winged Wonders," from Callaway Gardens Nature Notes; "Plants That Attract Hummingbirds in the Pacific Northwest," by Russell Link; "Some Plants for Hummers." by Tina Jones.

Resources

Local nurseries are a good source for many of the plants commonly grown in each region, but to find an assortment of less common ones, the imaginative hummingbird gardener searches mail-order outlets.

Kartuz Greenhouses
1408 Sunset Drive
Vista, CA 92083-6531
(619) 941-3613
*Columnea*s

Logee's Greenhouses
141 North Street
Danielson, CT 06239
(203) 774-8038
Tropicals and many others

National Wildflower Research Center
4801 La Crosse Avenue
Austin, TX 78739
(512) 292-4200
Provides information on places to obtain native plants

Park Seed Company
P.O. Box 31
Greenwood, SC 29648
(803) 223-8555

Plants of the Southwest
930 Baca Street
Santa Fe, NM 87501
(505) 983-1548
Penstemon, columbine, larkspur

Prairie Nursery
P.O. Box 306
Westfield, WI 53964
(608) 296-3679
Lobelia, Liatris, Physostegia

Sandy Mush Herb Nursery
316 Surrett Cove Road
Leicester, NC 28748-9622
(704) 683-2014
Salvia species, hyssops, bee balm, butterfly bush, coral bells, fuchsias, hostas, iris, lion's ear, *Lobelia*

Springhill Nursery
6523 North Galena Road
Peoria, IL 61632
(309) 689-3849

Stallings Nursery
910 Encinitas Boulevard
Encinitas, CA 92024
Flowering maples and *Iochroma*

Sunnybrook Farms Nursery
9448 Mayfield Road, P.O. Box 6
Chesterland, OH 44026
(216) 729-7232

Wayside Gardens
1 Garden Lane
Hodges, SC 29695
(800) 845-1124

Yucca Do Nursery at Peckerwood Gardens
P.O. Box 655
Waller, TX 77484
(409) 826-6363
*Salvia*s

Photography and Illustration Credits

William P. Bergen: 8, 9, 56, 84, 100, 122. **Rick and Nora Bowers:** 14, 118, 126, 127. **F. A. Cleland:** 60, 87. **Derek Fell:** 20, 27, 47, 68, 80, 130 (left and right), 133 (right), 134 (all images). **Clayton A. Fogle:** 29. **Maslowski Wildlife Productions:** 21, 31, 81, 92. **Charles W. Melton:** 12, 16, 24, 30, 33, 38, 43, 54, 63, 69, 76, 113, 114, 116, 128, 130 (center), 133 (left and center). **Anthony Mercieca:** 11, 18, 34, 45, 51, 55, 64, 72, 88, 96, 104, 105, 107, 108, 111, 117, 123, 125. **Betty Randall:** 48. **Saxon Holt:** 42. **Wendy Shattil and Bob Rozinski:** 10. **Stephen A. Shurtz:** 40, 52, 66, 79, 91, 103. **Robert A. Sutton:** 93, 110. **Sid and Shirley Rucker:** 120. **Luke Wade:** 37.

References and Further Reading

Aldrich, E.C. "Nesting of the Allen Hummingbird," *The Condor*, Vol. 47, 1945, pp. 137-148.

Allen, Arthur A. *American Bird Biographies*. Ithaca, New York: Comstock Publishing Company, 1934.

American Ornithologists' Union. *Check-list of North American Birds*, 6th edition, 1983.

Anderson, J.O. and G. Monson. "Berylline Hummingbirds nest in Arizona," *Continental Birdlife*, Vol 2, 1981, pp. 56-61.

Bailey, Liberty Hyde and Ethel Zoe Bailey. *Hortus Third, a Concise Dictionary of Plants Cultivated in the United States and Canada*. Initially compiled by Bailey and Bailey, revised and expanded by the staff of the Liberty Hyde Bailey Hortorium. New York: Macmillan Publishing Company, 1976.

Baltosser, William H. "Nectar Availability and Habitat Selection by Hummingbirds in Guadalupe Canyon," *The Wilson Bulletin*, Vol. 101, 1989, pp. 559-578.

Baltosser, William H. "Nesting Success and Productivity of Hummingbirds in Southwestern New Mexico and Southeastern Arizona," *The Wilson Bulletin*, Vol. 98, 1986, pp. 353-367.

Beal, Mary. "The Black-chinned Hummingbird," *Bird-Lore*, Vol. 35, 1933, pp. 96-97.

Bent, Arthur Cleveland. *Life Histories of North American Cuckoos, Goatsuckers, Hummingbirds and Their Allies, Part II*. United States National Museum Bulletin no. 176, 1940. Reprint. New York: Dover Publications, 1964.

Berger, Cynthia. "Donating Their Birdseed to Science," *National Wildlife*, December-January 1993, pp. 20-22.

Blakey, Louise G. *Our Hummingbirds*. Los Altos, California: Louise G. Blakey, 1985.

Bodine, Margaret L. "Holidays with Humming Birds," *National Geographic Magazine*, June 1928, pp. 731-742.

Botha, Celeste, Susan Cerulean and Donna Legare. *Planting a Refuge for Wildlife*. Tallahassee, Florida: Florida Game and Fresh Water Fish Commission and United States Department of Agriculture Soil Conservation Service, n.d.

Calder, William A. "Rufous Hummingbird," *The Birds of North America*. Philadelphia: The American Ornithologists' Union and The Academy of Natural Sciences of Philadelphia, 1993.

Calder, William A. and Lorene L. "Broad-tailed Hummingbird," *The Birds of North America*. Philadelphia: The American Ornithologists' Union and The Academy of Natural Sciences of Philadelphia, 1992.

Connor, Floyd, Peggy Latimer and Kit Muma. *Hummertime*. Elgin, Ontario: Hummertime, c/o Queen's University Biological Station, 1994-1995.

Dimmitt, Mark. "Desert Gardening," *Sonorensis*. Tucson: Arizona-Sonora Desert Museum, Vol. 13, No. 1, Winter 1993.

Dimmitt, Mark. "Landscaping for (and Against) Wildlife," *Sonorensis*. Tucson: Arizona-Sonora Desert Museum, Vol. 9, No. 3, Winter 1989.

Edgerton, Harold E. "Hummingbirds in Action," *National Geographic Magazine*, August 1947, pp. 220-232.

Ford, Alice. *The Bird Biographies of John James Audubon*. Selected and edited by Alice Ford. New York: The Macmillan Company, 1957.

Grinnell, Joseph. "Birds and mammals of the 1907 Alexander expedition to southeastern Alaska," *University of California Publ. Zool.*, Vol. 5, 1909, pp. 171-264.

Henderson, Carroll L. *Landscaping for Wildlife*. St. Paul: Minnesota Department of Natural Resources, 1987.

Hine, Jane L. "Observations on the ruby-throated hummingbird," *The Auk*, Vol. 11, pp. 253-254, 1894.

Holmes, Roger, ed. *Taylor's Guide to Natural Gardening*. New York: Houghton Mifflin Company, 1993.

Holmgren, Virginia C. *The Way of the Hummingbird*. Santa Barbara: Capra Press, 1986.

How to Attract Hummingbirds and Butterflies. San Ramon, California: Ortho Books, 1991.

"Hummingbirds take over bees' work," *Science News*, Vol. 146, November 19, 1994, p. 334.

Jardine, Sir William. *The Naturalists' Library*. Volumes 6-7. London/Edinburgh: W. H. Lizars [1833-1834?].

Johnsgard, Paul A. *The Hummingbirds of North America*. Washington, D.C.: Smithsonian Institution Press, 1983.

Kaufman, K. "Lucifer Hummingbird identification," *American Birds*, Vol. 46, pp. 491-494, 1992.

Kuban, Joseph F., and R.L. Neill. "Feeding ecology of hummingbirds in the highlands of the Chisos Mountains, Texas," *The Condor*, Vol. 82, 1980, pp. 180-185.

Lamb, Chester Converse. "Observations on the Xantus hummingbird," *The Condor*, Vol. 27, 1925, pp. 89-92.

Lowery, George H., Jr. *Louisiana Birds*. Baton Rouge: Louisiana State University Press, 1974.

Newfield, Nancy L. *Louisiana's Hummingbirds*. Baton Rouge: Louisiana Department of Wildlife and Fisheries, 1993.

Newfield, Nancy L. "Plant a Hummingbird Garden," *Birder's World*, March-April 1987, pp. 46-50.

Newfield, Nancy L. "When to Take Down Your Hummingbird Feeder," *Bird Watcher's Digest*, September-October 1989, pp. 80-83.

Oberholser, Harry C. *The Bird Life of Texas*. Austin: University of Texas Press, 1974.

Oviedo y Valdés, Gonzalo Fernández de. *De la Natural hystoria de las Indias*. Toledo, Spain, 1526.

Peterson, Roger Tory. *Birds Over America*. New York: Dodd, Mead and Company, 1964 (first edition, 1948).

Peterson, Roger Tory. *Favorite Audubon Birds of America*. New York: Crown Publishers, Inc., n.d.

Phillips, Allan R. "The Migration of Allen's and Other Hummingbirds," *The Condor*, Vol. 77, pp. 196-205, 1975.

Pope, Thomas, Neil Odenwald and Charles Fryling. *Attracting Birds to Southern Gardens*. Dallas: Taylor Publishing Co., 1993.

Ridgway, Robert. *United States geological exploration of the fortieth parallel*. Part 3: Ornithology, 1877.

Robertson, William B., Jr., and Glen E. Woolfenden. *Florida Bird Species: An Annotated List*. Gainesville, Florida: Florida Ornithological Society, 1992.

Scott, P.E. "A Closer Look: Lucifer Hummingbird," *Birding*, Vol. 25, pp. 245-251, 1993.

Scott, P.E. "Lucifer Hummingbird," *The Birds of North America*. Philadelphia: The American Ornithologists' Union and The Academy of Natural Sciences of Philadelphia, 1994.

Scott, S.L., ed. *Field Guide to the Birds of North America*. Second edition. Washington, D.C.: National Geographic Society, 1987.

Skutch, Alexander F. *The Life of the Hummingbird*. New York: Vineyard Books, 1973.

Skutch, Alexander F. *A Naturalist on a Tropical Farm*. Berkeley and Los Angeles: University of California Press, 1980.

Stiles, F.G. "Aggressive and Courtship Displays of the Male Anna's Hummingbird," *The Condor*, Vol. 84, pp. 208-225, 1982.

Stiles, F.G. "On the Field Identification of California Hummingbirds," *California Birds*, Vol. 2, pp. 41-54, 1971.

Stokes, Donald and Lillian. *The Hummingbird Book*. Boston: Little, Brown and Company, 1989.

Sunset Western Garden Book. Menlo Park, California: Lane Publishing Co., 1988.

Tekulsky, Mathew. *The Hummingbird Garden*. New York: Crown Publishers, Inc., 1990.

Toops, Connie. *Hummingbirds: Jewels in Flight*. Stillwater, Minnesota: Voyageur Press, Inc., 1992.

True, Dan. *Hummingbirds of North America*. Albuquerque: University of New Mexico Press, 1993.

Tyrrell, Esther Q., and Robert A. *Hummingbirds: Their Life and Behavior*. New York: Crown Publishers, Inc., 1985.

Wetmore, Alexander. "Seeking the Smallest Feathered Creatures," *National Geographic Magazine*, July 1932, pp. 64-89.

Wood, William. *New England's Prospects*. London: John Dawson, 1634. University Microfilms, English Books 1475-1640, Reel 980.

Index

Numbers in boldface refer to photographs; numbers in italics refer to hummingbird species descriptions.